Table of

PROBLEMS IN EUROPEAN CIVILIZATION

THE OUTBREAK
OF THE
FIRST WORLD WAR

Who or What Was Responsible?

THIRD EDITION

EDITED WITH AN INTRODUCTION BY

Dwight E. Lee

CLARK UNIVERSITY

D. C. HEATH AND COMPANY
Lexington, Massachusetts

THE OUTBREAK
OF THE FIRST WORLD WAR

Who or What Was Responsible?

Third Edition

Introduction

THE ORIGINS of the First World War have become a major historical problem not merely because the event seemed to be of great significance as a turning point in world history, but also, and perhaps more importantly, because the question of who was responsible, raised during the war and answered in the peace settlement, became a vital and passionately argued issue in both domestic and international politics.

By placing the blame for the war on Germany and its allies and thereby justifying reparations, the victorious powers supplied one of the major factors utilized by Hitler in his rise to power in Germany. The reaction to the Versailles verdict which occurred in the victorious countries as well as in Germany resulted in an attack upon Article 231 of the Versailles treaty in the name of "revisionism." Thus there arose a battle whose front extended from newspapers and popular magazines, through the offices of propagandists and politicians and the quieter studies of scholarly historians, to the halls of parliaments and the green baize tables of international conferences. By the middle of the 1930's the excited conflict of opinion had cooled down and the issues had receded into the background of political discussion as reparations payments stopped and Hitler achieved revision. The study of the problem, however, has inevitably continued, albeit at a slower and soberer pace until the revival of the war-guilt question in Germany in 1961 again created a furor in the historical world.

Before coming to that third phase of the problem, some general considerations are worth noting. First of all, for the historian the judgment of the peacemakers proved to be a boon because the Germans immediately undertook to refute the charges against their nation by publishing a huge collection of documents from their foreign office archives covering the period from 1871 to 1914. Since this action could not go unchallenged, other governments had to follow the German example and produce their records. As a result, and even though the publications of Italy and Russia are still incomplete, the historian has had at his disposal a vast store of primary source material with which to work. Thus, when normally the scholar would have had to wait at least a hundred years to get at the secrets of government offices, he has been embarrassed with the riches of documentary evidence for the backgrounds of the First World War. Of course, the first decade of the "revisionist" battle was fought without the complete body of primary sources, and that is one reason why study must go on if we are ever to assess the evidence and draw conclusions fairly.

Another reason for the continued study of this, as of other historical problems, is that viewpoints change and with them the questions which historians seek to answer. Article 231 of Versailles fixed the searchlight of the 1920's upon the question "Who was guilty?" As the smoke of the revisionist battle gradually drifted away, it became obvious that this was not a proper question for the historian because the answer would scarely contribute to a better understanding of historical processes nor help us to improve the chances of peaceful development today. For, even if Germany were guilty in 1914, it would be absurd to believe, especially after 1947, that by punishing and fettering Germany we could prevent war. As time went on, therefore, more and more attention was devoted to such questions as "What were the conditions that made war possible?" and "Why, when so many crises were solved peaceably between 1871 and 1914, did that of 1914 end in war?" The answers to such questions depend not only upon the bare record of the documents and other contemporary evidence, but also upon the conscious or unconscious assumptions which the student makes about economic, political, intellectual, and social factors in the formulation of policy and the making of decisions by national governments, because these assumptions help to determine what the historian will select and what he will reject from the overwhelming mass of evidence, and they help to determine what interpretation he will put upon the wording of his documents.

In the small space available in the following pages it is impossible to reproduce all the "key" documents, even for the short period of less than a month in the 1914 crisis which ended in war. Nor is it possible to give detailed interpretations of the exchanges which took place among the statesmen involved, for the most thorough of these studies run to volumes rather than pages. Therefore the selection of readings has been made in order to give (1) something of the flavor of the revisionist debate at its height in the twenties, (2) the principal viewpoints that emerged in the three decades that followed, and (3) a sample of the heated German controversy that arose in the sixties over Germany's guilt. The "Suggestions for Additional Reading" at the end will give some guidance to those who would like to get beneath the surface and examine the evidence for themselves.

Under Part I the report of 1919 made to the peace conference on the responsibility for the war of Germany and its allies appropriately begins the selection of readings, not only because it was the basis for Article 231 of the Versailles treaty, but also because it reflects the inevitably one-sided approach of the victors to the question of guilt as well as the comparative paucity of sources on which their judgment was based. Following the "Report" are four examples of revisionist literature of the 1920's.

Two German statements head the list. One of these is an early defense of Germany drawn up by Count Montgelas, who went to Versailles as a member of the German delegation in order to refute the charges against Germany and continued, through his editing of documents and his writings, to take a leading part in the drive to clear Germany of "guilt." Erich Brandenburg, an outstanding German historian, asserts a more moderate conclusion than that of the extreme revisionists and also introduces such factors in the background of 1914 as imperialism, nationalism, and the anachronistic structure of the Danubian monarchy, which the historian must inevitably assess. Harry Elmer Barnes, an American historian and sociologist, sets forth the extreme revisionist view held in the United States as well as in Germany, France, and Great Britain. The excerpt from Sidney Bradshaw Fay's *Origins* appropriately concludes this group of revisionist statements because he was the first in the United States to publish his inquiries in the spirit of scholarly investigation rather than that of political polemics and thus to reflect the more judicious temper of the late 1920's. It is unfortunate that the equally well-known publication by the outstanding historian Bernadotte E. Schmitt, *The Coming of the War,* does not lend itself to excerpting, because with the same documents as Fay had at hand he comes to opposite conclusions concerning war guilt.

Opening Part II and in contrast with the excited interpretations of the early revisionists is the balanced account of the July crisis by George Peabody Gooch, who was able to approach the subject with detachment and to utilize a more extensive body of documentary evidence than was available ten years before. The selection from his book *Before the War* not only narrates the story, but also conveys something of the flavor of the documents because of his many direct quotations.

Another kind of extreme "revisionism" from that of Montgelas or Barnes has existed since the early days of the First World War — the Marxist interpretation. Although the extract from K. Zilliacus, a British left-wing parliamentarian and writer, is not as violent or dogmatic as many of the Marxists have been, it nevertheless gives the view that the war is to be explained by economic rivalries, class interests, and the machinations of finance capital. On the other hand, there has emerged a counter-Marxist trend which discounts the importance of economic factors or denies the validity of economic determinism. Pierre Renouvin, the leading French historian of international affairs, while recognizing the importance of economic and social factors, not only throws doubt upon the notion that capitalist competition caused the war, but also calls attention to the personal element in diplomacy as well as to nationalism and the passions it aroused.

Since the rise of Hitler and the subsequent German attack upon Poland, there has been a revival of the German "war guilt" thesis. An example of present-day students who believe in German guilt is A. J. P. Taylor, a brilliant British historian who offers some challenging interpretations of German guilt and of other aspects of the problem, such as the significance of the alliance system, the relationship of Great Britain to the other powers in the 1914 crisis, and the meaning of balance of power. At the same time, the *Conclusions* of the French and German historians, designed to eliminate hate-perpetuating and nationalistic propaganda from history textbooks, offers an interesting recent agreement upon the interpretation of policies and events in 1914. Reflecting the results of many years of scholarly endeavor, these assertions must be regarded as perhaps more important for the effort to achieve Franco-German reconciliation and friendship than as a solution to the war guilt problem. Nevertheless they do embody interpretations which can be

validly upheld on the basis of present evidence.

Next, Raymond Aron well conveys the atmosphere of research in the fifties, and makes clear the position of the scholarly student for whom 1914 and its background is no "simple picture" but rather one of great complexity from which "storybook villains" are absent. He is not saying, however, that there is no problem for the student in the outbreak of the war, but rather that the reduction of general and immediate causes to black-and-white terms, to "guilty" and "guiltless," is to miss the point. There was no inevitable trend of events toward war, but rather the acts of sovereign states seeking what seemed to them at the time to be in their best interest. Alliances and armaments, pursued for defense, proved to be the means of creating tension; the nationalist ambition of a small Balkan state, backed by a great power, threatened the existence of an historic empire, supported by another great power. The alliances and alignments guaranteed that the crisis would be Europe-wide. In this situation, the decisions of Austria-Hungary and Germany on the one hand, and of Russia on the other, involved fateful consequences.

Finally, Bernadotte E. Schmitt's pamphlet on *The Origins of the First World War*, published in 1958, also reflects the calmer judgments of the fifties rather than the early heated controversy over "war guilt" in which he had taken part. His pamphlet is noteworthy for its excellent short summary of the backgrounds of the war (in the main omitted from the extracts reprinted below). In this summary he emphasizes the drive for self-determination as the most important single underlying cause of the war, while agreeing with Renouvin and others that economic rivalry was not important. In dealing with the 1914 crisis, he differs from such interpreters as S. B. Fay in asserting that Berlin did not unwittingly give Vienna freedom of action against Serbia, but carefully calculated the risks and knew well what it was doing. Moreover, he plays up the eagerness for war and the intervention of Moltke, Chief of the German General Staff, at the end of July to a greater extent than the revisionists do. On the other hand, while admitting that Russia ordered general mobilization in the knowledge that it would provoke German mobilization, he disregards the emphasis which many revisionists put upon the French desire for revenge and plays down the French encouragement of Russia. In his conclusion he finds with other recent writers that the issue in 1914 was the "balance of power," and that the alliance system, designed for defense, converted "a local conflict into a general war."

In Part III, two statements illustrate the revived war-guilt debate in Germany, but before commenting upon them, something of the background needs to be sketched. The first, full-length, thoroughly documented reassertion of German war guilt was published in three volumes by Luigi Albertini, Italian journalist and Senator, in 1942–43. His work was translated into English and edited by Isabella M. Massey as *The Origins of the War of 1914,* in three volumes, 1952–57. Neither the Italian nor the English editions were taken seriously in Germany until Fritz Fischer, first in a periodical article and then in his book, *Griff nach der Weltmacht* [*Grab for World Power*], in 1961 startled the German historical profession and public by affirming Albertini's conclusion that Germany was guilty of starting the war, as part of his exposition of Germany's aggressive economic war aims. The impact of his book can be understood only if we recall that German innocence and the notion that Germany had fought defensively in the war had become truths that no German before had dared to challenge. The furor which arose over Fischer's position has been dubbed the "Fischer controversy."[1]

Thus, Fischer's interpretation of Germany's responsibility for the outbreak of the war in 1914 appropriately opens Part III on "German War Guilt Revived." His exposition parallels, but lacks the fulness and richness of detail of Albertini's study which, unfortunately, does not lend itself to excerpting for reproduction here.

Three groups of German critics and commentators who have participated in the "Fischer controversy" may be distinguished: those who cling to the traditional view of German innocence and flatly deny the validity of Fischer's thesis, those who fully accept and expand upon it, and those who admit that the older war-guilt literature needs revision but reject Fischer's reconstruction of the July crisis. Among the last is Gerhard Ritter, one of whose critical reviews of Fischer's book is reprinted in part below. He contends that Fischer has misinterpreted the sources in his determination to prove a thesis, but does not attempt to offer a full-length exposition of his own.

Thus far, aside from a few pieces of newly discovered source material, the German controversy has not significantly added to the substance of the debate nor changed the issues and viewpoints concerning the outbreak of the war that emerged in the literature of the twenties and thirties, excepting, perhaps, to cast Bethmann Hollweg in a new light — a point which the Ritter selection briefly touches upon. Furthermore, since as yet the responsibility of other powers has not been dealt with in the light of the war-aims approach which Fischer has applied to Germany, the ultimate significance of the reassertion of German guilt remains to be assessed in the context of the total problem of why the war broke out when it did.

[1] For a short summary of the controversy and the personalities involved, see Imanuel Geiss, *July 1914* (New York, 1967), pp. 9–15; and for a description of the means by which the German foreign office had promoted the revisionist thesis in the 1920's, see Geiss, "Outbreak of the First World War and German War Aims," *Journal of Contemporary History,* I, 3 (1966), 75–79; or *1914,* edited by Walter Laqueur and George L. Mosse (Harper Torchbook, New York, 1966), pp. 71–77.

The challenge to the student historian therefore remains. In examining the conflict of opinion represented in the selections offered here and pursuing his study further, he may find his inquiry more meaningful if he asks himself such questions as these: Upon what assumptions and within what frames of reference were the statesmen of 1914 making their decisions? What were the choices before them? Why did they make the decisions that they did? Given the system of independent, sovereign national states, each seeking ultimately its own security and well-being, could greater intelligence, more determination to avoid the risks of war, or speedier and franker statements of positions have averted bloodshed? Or were the issues such that they could not be resolved by peaceful means because they touched upon "vital" national interests? And, despite Aron and others, were there "villains" after all?

The Principal Proper Names

Appearing in the Readings

AEHRENTHAL, ALOIS, BARON (later, COUNT LEXA), Austro-Hungarian Minister for Foreign Affairs, 1906 to February, 1912.

BALLPLATZ, the location in Vienna of the Ministry of Foreign Affairs and hence a synonym for it.

BENCKENDORFF, ALEXANDER, COUNT, Russian Ambassador to Great Britain, 1903–1916.

BERCHTOLD, LEOPOLD VON, COUNT, Austro-Hungarian Minister for Foreign Affairs, February, 1912 to 1915.

BETHMANN-HOLLWEG, DR. THEOBALD VON, Chancellor of the German Empire, May, 1909 to 1917.

BUCHANAN, SIR GEORGE WILLIAM, British Ambassador to Russia, 1910–1918.

BÜLOW, BERNHARD VON, PRINCE, German Minister for Foreign Affairs, 1897–1900, and Chancellor, 1900 to May, 1909.

BUNSEN, SIR MAURICE, British Ambassador in Vienna, 1913–1914.

CAILLAUX, JOSEPH, leading Radical Socialist deputy; French Premier, June, 1911 to January, 1912.

CAMBON, JULES, French Ambassador in Berlin, 1907–1914.

CAMBON, PAUL, French Ambassador in London, 1898–1920.

CAMPBELL-BANNERMAN, SIR HENRY, British Prime Minister, 1905–1908.

CAROL I, King of Rumania, 1881 to October 2, 1914.

CHAMBERLAIN, JOSEPH, British statesman; Secretary of State for the Colonies, 1895–1903.

CONRAD VON HÖTZENDORF, FRANZ, BARON (later, COUNT), Austro-Hungarian Chief of the General Staff, 1906–1911 (Dec.), 1912 (Dec.)–1917.

DELCASSÉ, THÉOPHILE, French Minister for Foreign Affairs, 1898 to June, 1905.

DOBROROLSKI, SERGEI K., Russian general; Chief of the Mobilization Section of the general staff, 1914.

FRANCIS FERDINAND, ARCHDUKE, Heir apparent (1896–1914) to the throne of Austria-Hungary.

FRANCIS JOSEPH I, Emperor of Austria (1848–1916) and King of Hungary (1867–1916).

GIESL, WLADIMIR, BARON VON GIESLINGEN, Austro-Hungarian Minister to Serbia, November, 1913 to July 25, 1914.

GOSCHEN, SIR WILLIAM EDWARD, British Ambassador to Germany, November, 1908 to 1914.

GREY, SIR EDWARD (later, VISCOUNT GREY OF FALLODON), British Secretary of State for Foreign Affairs, December, 1905 to 1916.

HOYOS, LADISLAUS, COUNT, Secretary for Balkan Affairs at the Austro-Hungarian Ministry of Foreign Affairs.

IZVOLSKY [ISWOLSKI], ALEXANDER PETROVICH, Russian Foreign Minister, May, 1906 to September, 1910; Ambassador to France, 1910–1917.

JAGOW, GOTTLIEB VON, German Secretary of State for Foreign Affairs, 1913–1916.

JAURÈS, JEAN, leader of the French Socialist party, who was assassinated in July, 1914.

LICHNOWSKY, KARL MAX VON, PRINCE, German Ambassador to Great Britain, 1912–1914.

MOLTKE, HELMUTH J. L. VON, Chief of the German General Staff, 1906–1914.

MUSULIN, VON GOMIRJE, ALEXANDER, head of the chancery at the Austro-Hungarian Ministry of Foreign Affairs.

NICOLSON, SIR ARTHUR (later, LORD CARNOCK), British Ambassador to Russia, 1906–1910; Permanent Under-Secretary of State for Foreign Affairs, 1910–1916.

PALÉOLOGUE, MAURICE, *French Ambassador to Russia, January, 1914 to 1917.*

PASHICH [PASHITCH], NIKOLA, *Serbian Prime Minister, 1912–1919.*

POINCARÉ, RAYMOND, *French Premier, January, 1912 to February, 1913; President of the French Republic, February, 1913 to 1920.*

POURTALÈS, FRIEDRICH VON, COUNT, *German Ambassador to Russia, 1907–1914.*

QUAI D'ORSAY, *the location in Paris of the Ministry of Foreign Affairs and hence a synonym for it.*

SALISBURY, ROBERT CECIL, MARQUESS OF, *British Secretary of State for Foreign Affairs and Premier several times until his retirement in July, 1902.*

SAN GIULIANO, ANTONINO, MARQUIS OF, *Italian Minister for Foreign Affairs, 1910 to October, 1914.*

SAZONOV [SAZONOFF], SERGEI D., *Russian Minister for Foreign Affairs, September, 1910 to 1916.*

SCHILLING, MAURICE F., BARON, *head of the Chancery of the Russian Ministry of Foreign Affairs, 1912–1914.*

SCHLIEFFEN, ALFRED VON, COUNT, *German Chief of the General Staff, 1891–1905.*

SZÖGÉNYI, LASZLO, COUNT, *Austro-Hungarian Ambassador to Germany, 1892–1914.*

TIRPITZ, ALFRED VON, *German Admiral, Navy Minister, 1898–1916.*

TISZA, STEPHEN, COUNT, *Hungarian Premier, 1913–1917.*

TSCHIRSCHKY UND BÖGENDORFF, HEINRICH LEONHARD VON, *German Ambassador to Austria-Hungary, 1907–1916.*

VIVIANI, RENÉ, *French Premier and Minister for Foreign Affairs, June to August, 1914.*

WILHELMSTRASSE, *location in Berlin of the German Foreign Office and hence a synonym for it.*

WOLFF, THEODOR, *German journalist; editor of the* Berliner Tageblatt *in 1914.*

ZIMMERMANN, ALFRED, *German Under-Secretary of State for Foreign Affairs, 1911–1916.*

The Conflict of Opinion

Germany and her allies were the aggressors

"The Allied and Associated Governments affirm and Germany accepts the responsibility of Germany and her allies for causing all the loss and damage to which the Allied and Associated Governments and their nationals have been subjected as a consequence of the war imposed upon them by the aggression of Germany and her allies."

— *Article 231 of the Treaty of Versailles*

France and Russia willed the war

"The Franco-Russian Alliance concluded by 1894 was transformed into an offensive organization following 1912 through the cooperation of Izvolski and Poincaré. Both recognized that the chief objects of Russian and French foreign policy, the seizure of the Straits and the return of Alsace-Lorraine, could be realized only through a general European war. . . . When the assassination [of Francis Ferdinand] came, the French and Russians recognized that the impending clash between Austria and Serbia would constitute a highly appropriate episode over which to bring about the desired conflict. . . . In estimating the order of guilt of the various countries we may safely say that the only direct and immediate responsibility for the World War falls upon Serbia, France and Russia, with the guilt about equally distributed."

— Harry Elmer Barnes

No criminals, either men or nations

"The inquiry into political responsibility carries with it no authority to banish as criminals either men or nations. But inquiry does clarify the significance and the origins of the war."

— Raymond Aron

No one wanted war; all accepted it

"The documents do not permit attributing a premeditated desire for a European war on the part of any government or people in 1914. Distrust was at a peak and ruling circles were dominated by the idea that war was inevitable. Each one accused the other of aggressive intentions; each accepted the risk of war and saw its hope of security in the alliance system and the development of armament."

— *Conclusion of French and German Historians, 1951*

I. VERSAILLES: RIGHT OR WRONG?

Report Presented to the Preliminary
Peace Conference (1919)

COMMISSION ON WAR GUILT

"The Commission on the Responsibility of the Authors of the War and on Enforcement of Penalties," to give its full title, was created at the plenary session of the Paris Peace Conference of January 25, 1919. Two representatives of each of the five Great Powers (The United States, France, Great Britain, Italy, and Japan) and one each from Belgium, Greece, Poland, Roumania, and Serbia made up its membership. United States Secretary of State Robert Lansing was chosen chairman of the Commission which made its report toward the end of March. The Conference, at its plenary session of May 6, 1919, unanimously adopted the report although both the United States and Japan added reservations. Only the first chapter of the report has been reprinted below. Note that most of the sources used as a basis for the report are documents, often carefully edited, which the belligerents issued in the various "color books" shortly after the outbreak of the war.

O N THE QUESTION of the responsibility of the authors of the war, the Commission, after having examined a number of official documents relating to the origin of the World War, and to the violations of neutrality and of frontiers which accompanied its inception, has determined that the responsibility for it lies wholly upon the Powers which declared war in pursuance of a policy of aggression, the concealment of which gives to the origin of this war the character of a dark conspiracy against the peace of Europe.

This responsibility rests first on Germany and Austria, secondly on Turkey and Bulgaria. The responsibility is made all the graver by reason of the violation by Germany and Austria of the neutrality of Belgium and Luxemburg, which they themselves had guaranteed. It is increased, with regard to both France and Serbia, by the

violation of their frontiers before the declaration of war.

PREMEDITATION OF THE WAR:
GERMANY AND AUSTRIA

Many months before the crisis of 1914 the German Emperor had ceased to pose as the champion of peace. Naturally believing in the overwhelming superiority of his Army, he openly showed his enmity towards France. General von Moltke said to the King of the Belgians: "This time the matter must be settled." In vain the King protested. The Emperor and his Chief of Staff remained no less fixed in their attitude.[1]

On the 28th of June, 1914, occurred the assassination at Serajevo of the heir-apparent of Austria. "It is the act of a little group

[1] [French] Yellow Book; Mr. Cambon to Mr. Pichon, Berlin, November 22, 1913.

From the *German White Book Concerning the Responsibility of the Authors of the War* (New York, 1924), pp. 15–21. Used with the permission of the Carnegie Endowment for International Peace.

of madmen," said Francis Joseph.[2] The act, committed as it was by a subject of Austria-Hungary on Austro-Hungarian territory, could in no wise compromise Serbia, which very correctly expressed its condolences[3] and stopped public rejoicings in Belgrade. If the Government of Vienna thought that there was any Serbian complicity, Serbia was ready[4] to seek out the guilty parties. But this attitude failed to satisfy Austria and still less Germany, who, after their first astonishment had passed, saw in this royal and national misfortune a pretext to initiate war.

At Potsdam a "decisive consultation" took place on the 5th of July, 1914.[5] Vienna and Berlin decided upon this plan: "Vienna will send to Belgrade a very emphatic ultimatum with a very short limit of time."[6]

The Bavarian Minister, von Lerchenfeld, said in a confidential dispatch dated the 18th of July, 1914, the facts stated in which have never been officially denied: "It is clear that Serbia cannot accept the demands, which are inconsistent with the dignity of an independent state."[7] Count Lerchenfeld reveals in this report that, at the time it was made, the ultimatum to Serbia had been jointly decided upon by the Governments of Berlin and Vienna; that they were waiting to send it until President Poincaré and Mr. Viviani should have left for St. Petersburg; and that no illusions were cherished, either at Berlin or Vienna, as to the consequences which this threatening measure would involve. It was perfectly well known that war would be the result.

The Bavarian Minister explains, moreover, that the only fear of the Berlin Government was that Austria-Hungary might hesitate and draw back at the last minute,

and that on the other hand Serbia, on the advice of France and Great Britain, might yield to the pressure put upon her. Now, "the Berlin Government considers that war is necessary." Therefore, it gave full powers to Count Berchtold, who instructed the Ballplatz on the 18th of July, 1914, to negotiate with Bulgaria to induce her to enter into an alliance and to participate in the war.

In order to mask this understanding, it was arranged that the Emperor should go for a cruise in the North Sea, and that the Prussian Minister of War should go for a holiday, so that the Imperial Government might pretend that events had taken it completely by surprise.

Austria suddenly sent Serbia an ultimatum that she had carefully prepared in such a way as to make it impossible to accept. Nobody could be deceived; "the whole world understands that this ultimatum means war."[8] According to Mr. Sazonoff, "Austria-Hungary wanted to devour Serbia."[9]

Mr. Sazonoff asked Vienna for an extension of the short time-limit of forty-eight hours given by Austria to Serbia for the most serious decision in its history.[10] Vienna refused the demand. On the 24th and 25th of July, England and France multiplied their efforts to persuade Serbia to satisfy the Austro-Hungarian demands. Russia threw in her weight on the side of conciliation.[11]

Contrary to the expectation of Austria-Hungary and Germany, Serbia yielded. She agreed to all the requirements of the ultimatum, subject to the single reservation that, in the judicial inquiry which she would commence for the purpose of seeking out the guilty parties, the participation of Austrian officials would be kept within the limits assigned by international law. "If the Austro-Hungarian Government is not satisfied with this," Serbia declared she

[2] Message to his people.
[3] Serbian Blue Book, p. 30.
[4] Yellow Book, No. 15; Mr. Cambon to Mr. Bienvenu-Martin, July 21, 1914.
[5] Lichnowsky memoir. ["The Lichnowsky Memorandum," International Conciliation, No. 127 (June, 1918), 246–351.]
[6] Dr. Muehlon's memoir. [The Disclosures from Germany, tr. and ed. by Munroe Smith (New York, 1918), 183–227.]
[7] Report of July 18, 1914.

[8] Lichnowsky memoir.
[9] Austro-Hungarian Red Book, No. 16.
[10] [British] Blue Book, No. 26.
[11] Yellow Book, No. 36; Blue Book, Nos. 12, 46, 55, 65, 94, 118.

was ready "to submit to the decision of the Hague Tribunal."[12]

"A quarter of an hour before the expiration of the time limit," at 5:45 on the 25th, Mr. Pashitch, the Serbian Minister for Foreign Affairs, delivered this reply to Baron Giesl, the Austro-Hungarian Minister.

On Mr. Pashitch's return to his own office he found awaiting him a letter from Baron Giesl saying that he was not satisfied with the reply. At 6:30 the latter had left Belgrade, and even before he had arrived at Vienna, the Austro-Hungarian Government had handed his passports to Mr. Yovanovitch, the Serbian Minister, and had prepared thirty-three mobilization proclamations, which were published on the following morning in the *Budapesti Kozlöni*, the official gazette of the Hungarian Government. On the 27th Sir Maurice de Bunsen telegraphed to Sir Edward Grey: "This country has gone wild with joy at the prospect of war with Serbia."[13] At midday on the 28th Austria declared war on Serbia. On the 29th the Austrian army commenced the bombardment of Belgrade, and made its dispositions to cross the frontier.

The reiterated suggestions of the Entente Powers with a view to finding a peaceful solution of the dispute only produced evasive replies on the part of Berlin or promises of intervention with the Government of Vienna without any effectual steps being taken.

On the 24th of July Russia and England asked that the Powers should be granted a reasonable delay in which to work in concert for the maintenance of peace. Germany did not join in this request.[14]

On the 25th of July Sir Edward Grey proposed mediation by four Powers (England, France, Italy and Germany). France[15] and Italy[16] immediately gave their concurrence. Germany[17] refused, alleging that it was not a question of mediation but of arbitration, as the conference of the four Powers was called to make proposals, not to decide.

On the 26th of July Russia proposed to negotiate directly with Austria. Austria refused.[18]

On the 27th of July England proposed a European conference. Germany refused.[19]

On the 29th of July Sir Edward Grey asked the Wilhelmstrasse to be good enough to "suggest any method by which the influence of the four Powers could be used together to prevent a war between Austria and Russia."[20] She was asked herself to say what she desired.[21] Her reply was evasive.[22]

On the same day, the 29th of July, the Czar dispatched to the Emperor William II a telegram suggesting that the Austro-Serbian problem should be submitted to the Hague Tribunal. This suggestion received no reply. This important telegram does not appear in the German White Book. It was made public by the Petrograd *Official Gazette* (January, 1915).

The Bavarian Legation, in a report dated the 31st of July, declared its conviction that the efforts of Sir Edward Grey to preserve peace would not hinder the march of events.[23]

As early as the 21st of July German mobilization had commenced by the recall of a certain number of classes of the reserve,[24] then of German officers in Switzerland,[25] and finally of the Metz garrison on the 25th of July.[26] On the 26th of July the German Fleet was called back from Norway.[27]

---

[12] Yellow Book, No. 46.
[13] Blue Book, No. 41.
[14] Russian Orange Book, No. 4; Yellow Book, No. 43.
[15] Yellow Book, No. 70.
[16] *Ibid.*, No. 72; Blue Book, No. 49.
[17] Blue Book, No. 43.
[18] Yellow Book, No. 54.
[19] *Ibid.*, Nos. 68 and 73.
[20] *Ibid.*, No. 97; Blue Book, No. 84.
[21] Blue Book, No. 111.
[22] Yellow Book, Nos. 97, 98, and 109.
[23] Second report of Count Lerchenfeld, Bavarian plenipotentiary at Berlin, published on the instructions of Kurt Eisner.
[24] Yellow Book, No. 15.
[25] July 23, *ibid.*, No. 60.
[26] *Ibid.*, No. 106.
[27] *Ibid.*, No. 58.

The Entente did not relax its conciliatory efforts, but the German Government systematically brought all its attempts to nought. When Austria consented for the first time on the 31st of July to discuss the contents of the Serbian note with the Russian Government and the Austro-Hungarian Ambassador received orders to "converse" with the Russian Minister of Foreign Affairs,[28] Germany made any negotiation impossible by sending her ultimatum to Russia. Prince Lichnowsky wrote that "a hint from Berlin would have been enough to decide Count Berchtold to content himself with a diplomatic success and to declare that he was satisfied with the Serbian reply, but this hint was not given. *On the contrary they went forward towards war.*"[29]

On the 1st of August the German Emperor addressed a telegram to the King of England[30] containing the following sentence: "The troops on my frontier are, at this moment, being kept back by telegraphic and telephonic orders from crossing the French frontier." Now, war was not declared till two days after that date, and as the German mobilization orders were issued on that same day, the 1st of August, it follows that, as a matter of fact, the German Army had been mobilized and concentrated in pursuance of previous orders.

The attitude of the Entente nevertheless remained still to the very end so conciliatory that, at the very time at which the German fleet was bombarding Libau, Nicholas II gave his word of honor to William II that Russia would not undertake any aggressive action during the *pourparlers*,[31] and that when the German troops commenced their march across the French frontier Mr. Viviani telegraphed to all the French Ambassadors "we must not stop working for accommodation."

On the 3d of August Mr. von Schoen went to the Quai d'Orsay with the declaration of war against France. Lacking a real cause of complaint, Germany alleged, in her declaration of war, that bombs had been dropped by French aeroplanes in various districts in Germany. This statement was entirely false. Moreover, it was either later admitted to be so[32] or no particulars were ever furnished by the German Government.

Moreover, in order to be manifestly above reproach, France was careful to withdraw her troops ten kilometers from the German frontier. Notwithstanding this precaution, numerous officially established violations of French territory preceded the declaration of war.[33]

The provocation was so flagrant that Italy, herself a member of the Triple Alliance, did not hesitate to declare that in view of the aggressive character of the war the *casus foederis* ceased to apply.[34]

CONCLUSIONS

1. *The war was premeditated by the Central Powers together with their Allies, Turkey and Bulgaria, and was the result of acts deliberately committed in order to make it unavoidable.*

2. *Germany, in agreement with Austria-Hungary, deliberately worked to defeat all the many conciliatory proposals made by the Entente Powers and their repeated efforts to avoid war.*

[28] Blue Book, No. 133; Red Book, No. 55.

[29] Lichnowsky memoir, 41.

[30] [German] White Book, Annex 32; Yellow Book, Annex II *bis*, No. 2.

[31] Telegram from Nicholas II to William II; Yellow Book. No. 6, Annex V.

[32] Statement of the municipality of Nüremberg, dated April 3, 1916.

[33] (a) Patrols of various strengths crossed the French frontier at fifteen points, one on the 30th of July at Xures, eight on the 2d of August, and the others on the 3d of August, before war was declared.
The French troops lost one killed and several wounded. The enemy left on French territory four killed, one of whom was an officer, and seven prisoners. (b) At Suarce, on the 2d of August, the enemy carried off nine inhabitants, twenty-five horses, and three carriages. (c) Four incursions by German dirigibles took place between the 25th of July and the 1st of August. (d) Finally, German aeroplanes flew over Lunéville on the 3d of August, before the declaration of war, and dropped six bombs. (Yellow Book, Nos. 106, 136, 139, etc.)

[34] Yellow Book, No. 124.

The Case for the Central Powers

COUNT MAX MONTGELAS

Count Montgelas was a pioneer in revisionism, since he assisted in editing the famous "Kautsky Documents" (4 v., Berlin, 1919), representing the first attempt under the new German Republic to make known a more complete story of Germany's pre-war diplomacy than was afforded in the official "White Book" on the outbreak of war, and he was a member of the German Commission sent to Versailles to investigate the responsibility for the war. He participated in drawing up and signing the German response to the accusations of war guilt. After the conclusion of peace, he devoted himself almost entirely to the study of the backgrounds of the war, editing documents, writing articles and books, and pleading for a reversal of the Versailles verdict.

SEVENTEEN CONCLUSIONS

1

GERMANY PURSUED no aim either in Europe or elsewhere which could only be achieved by means of war.

Austria-Hungary's only aim was to maintain the *status quo*. Her first intention of rectifying her frontiers at Serbia's expense was immediately abandoned at Germany's instance, and even Sazonoff was convinced of her territorial *désintéressement* by her definite statements (A III. 19).

France aimed at recovering Alsace Lorraine, and many leading French politicians also hoped to annex the Saar basin, whilst Russia aspired to possession of Constantinople and the Straits, both Powers knowing well that these aims could not be achieved without a European war.

2

Germany's preparations for war were on a considerably smaller scale than those made by France, having regard to the political constellation, her geographical position, the extent of her unprotected frontiers, and the number of her population. From 1913 onwards, even her actual numerical peace strength was less, in respect of white troops, quite apart from the steadily increasing strength of the French coloured troops.

As compared with Russia's armaments, those of Austria-Hungary were absolutely inadequate.

The Franco-Russian allies were far superior to the Central Powers as regards the amount of war material, as well as of man power at their disposal.

3

It was a political mistake to construct a German battle fleet, instead of completing the naval defences, but even in London the proportion of ten to sixteen Dreadnoughts finally proposed by Germany was not regarded as a menace.

4

Even after Bismarck's time the German Empire repeatedly omitted to take advan-

From Count Max Montgelas, *The Case for the Central Powers* (London, 1925), Part III, Section 15, pp. 200–203. Translated by Constance Vesey. Reprinted by permission of George Allen & Unwin Ltd.

tage of favourable opportunities for a war of prevention.

5

The Russian suggestion of the first Hague Conference was not based on pure love of peace. All the Great Powers, without exception, were most sceptical as regards the question of reducing armaments; the Russian proposal of 1899 was unanimously rejected, and public opinion in France strongly opposed Campbell-Bannerman's 1907 suggestion.

Neither at the first nor the second Hague Conference was any proposal to adjust serious international conflicts, affecting the honour and vital interests of a nation, brought forward or supported by any Great Power.

6

The world war was not decided upon at Potsdam on the 5th of July, 1914; Germany merely assented to Austria's going to war with Serbia.

The possibility that the Austro-Serbian war, like others — the Boer, Moroccan, Tripolitan, and Balkan wars — might lead to further complications, was well weighed, but the risk was thought very small, in view of the special provocation.

7

After the publication of the Serbian reply, Germany no longer thought war advisable, even against Serbia, and only favoured strictly limited military operations, which were considered justifiable, even in London.

8

It is true that Germany did not support the proposal to extend the time limit, and rejected the idea of a conference. She not only, however, accepted every other proposal of mediation which came from London, but proposed on her own initiative the two most suitable methods of negotiation, namely, direct conversations between Vienna and St. Petersburg, and the idea of not going beyond Belgrade, which was adopted by Grey.

Sazonoff's first formula was considered unacceptable, even in London, and the second was far worse than the first.

9 .

An understanding had almost been reached by the methods Germany had been the first to propose, namely, direct discussions between Vienna and St. Petersburg, and limiting the military operations against Serbia, when the Russian mobilization suddenly tore the threads asunder.

10

The leading men knew just as well in Paris and St. Petersburg as in Berlin, that this mobilization must inevitably lead to war.

Viviani telegraphed to London on the 1st of August that the one who first orders general mobilization is the aggressor, and he saddled Germany with this responsibility, knowing that the accusation was false.

11

France did not advise moderation in St. Petersburg during the crisis. Finding that the first attempt to do so had annoyed Sazonoff, the French Government refrained from taking any further steps in this direction.

12

France not only did not advise Russia against ordering general mobilization, but gave surreptitious advice as to how she could carry on her military preparations secretly without provoking Germany to take timely countermeasures.

13

Russia was the first Power to order general mobilization.

France was the first Power to inform another Power officially of her decision to take part in a European war.

14

England was never as firm in advising moderation in St. Petersburg as Germany in giving this advice to Vienna.

Unlike other British diplomats, Sir Edward Grey only realized the meaning of the Russian mobilization when it was too late, and St. Petersburg was no longer willing to put a stop to it.

15

Germany's premature declaration of war on Russia was a political error, which can be accounted for by the immense danger of the position on two fronts; her declaration of war on France was a pure formality.

The decisive event was not this or that declaration of war, but the action which made the declaration of war inevitable, and this action was Russia's general mobilization.

16

England declared war on Germany because she did not consider it compatible with her interests that France should be defeated a second time. Belgian interests, and the treaty of 1839, which Lord Salisbury had been prepared to sacrifice in 1887, were the reasons adduced to make it popular.

Over and above this, the naval agreement of 1912 with France compelled England to abandon her neutrality before Belgium's neutrality was violated.

17

Greater diplomatic skill was shown by the Entente than by the Triple Alliance Powers.

By her false statements regarding Germany's preparations for war, particularly regarding the alleged priority of the German mobilization, by magnifying insignificant incidents on the frontier into invasions of French territory, and by withdrawing her covering troops to a distance of ten kilometres from the frontier,[1] France created the prior condition in London, which Benckendorff had indicated, as far back as at the end of 1912, as necessary for England's intervention. An impression was produced in London that "the opponents of the Entente were the aggressors."[2]

---

[1] As to this *ruse,* to deceive public opinion, vide Part IV, sect. 8, pp. 217 ff.

[2] Siebert [B. de, *Diplomatische Aktenstücke zur Geschichte der Ententepolitik der Vorkriegsjahre* (Berlin, 1921)], p. 588.

Conclusion: The Causes of the War

ERICH BRANDENBURG

Professor at Leipzig University and one of the leading historians of Germany, Erich Brandenburg gained permission to study the archives of the German foreign office in preparing his book on the backgrounds of the war of 1914. His focus was German policy, and his purpose was to find out what had gone wrong after the resignation of Bismarck that produced a situation in which Germany, after having once enjoyed diplomatic hegemony on the continent, had found herself in a war from which she emerged a defeated power. Though his attitude toward war guilt was revisionist, he nevertheless found much to criticize in German policy. His conclusions, which follow, reflect a cooler judgment than that of many contemporary revisionists.

THE CRIME of Sarajevo brought out the Vienna plan for a final reckoning with Serbia. It was thought that the only way to save the threatened existence of the Monarchy was to give proof to the world of its vitality by administering an exemplary chastisement to this dangerous neighbour. We thought that we ought not to hold Austria back, and we hoped by the old methods to prevent Russia from intervening. We underestimated the dangers of that policy, and were ourselves obsessed by the feeling that if the great reckoning must come it was perhaps as well it should come now and for this cause. So we landed ourselves in a plight from which, after our vain efforts at the last moment to extricate Austria, there was no longer any outlet but war.

German policy during these years has earned many and heavy reproaches. It can justly be accused of short-sightedness, lack of method, want of forethought and of understanding of the psychology of other peoples; we can blame Germany's vacillation and her sudden recklessness, as in the Morocco question, for instance. But no one can maintain with any show of reason that at any given time she either wished for war or strove to bring it about. Had Germany really wanted war, no more favourable time could have been found than during and after the Russo-Japanese War. Russia was then incapable of action, France and England inadequately equipped, and the Entente only recently founded. Had we wanted a preventive war all the chances were in our favour then and up till 1909. The General Staff, as in duty bound, had called attention to that fact. But this possibility was never seriously entertained by our Government, and even in 1909, when Austria was considering an invasion of Serbia, it worked consistently for peace. Perhaps it would have been wiser to attack boldly then, but that was not done because of the desire not to break the peace unless compelled. In spite of all the sounding words that have been spoken, our policy was, in fact, too anxious and too peace-loving rather than too militant. We never wanted to win at the expense of others, but

From Erich Brandenburg, *From Bismarck to the World War* (Translated by Anne Elizabeth Adams; London, 1927), pp. 518–23. Reprinted by permission of Oxford University Press.

only and always to share with them and alongside of them in the apportioning of the earth.

Can as much be said of the other Powers concerned?

As regards England, so far as we can learn from the sources at present available, no one in England really wanted war. The view so widely held in Germany that Britain engineered the war in order to destroy our economic competition, which was becoming increasingly dangerous to her, has little justification. But across the Channel they did fear our growing political and military power; they felt their own supremacy and security threatened by the growth of our battle fleet, and they credited us with the intention of seizing the hegemony of the Continent of Europe. In order to secure themselves against such possibilities and to prevent us from occupying permanently the position of arbiter, the Entente was founded when the alliance with Germany failed. English statesmen intended it to be a means of maintaining the balance of power and of keeping Germany's might and ambition within due bounds; there is no indication that it was originally intended as an instrument of war. Undoubtedly in London at the outset they underestimated the danger of dividing Europe into two hostile leagues. When they did realize it, they sought to get into touch again with Germany without surrendering the Entente, and so in a manner to recover their supremacy over the parties. But they were by that time too closely bound to the one group, and they had not the power to direct the policy of their allies entirely in the path which they desired. As they were convinced that in a war in which England took no part Germany would be victorious and become master of Europe, they were forced, if the war could not be prevented, to take sides with France and Russia; otherwise they would be faced by the very situation to escape which the Entente had been founded. So it was that England too was ultimately dependent on the decision of her allies, without wishing it, and without

clearly realizing it. The fact that Grey himself felt bound to the Entente policy was naturally of great significance. But at the critical moment he might have been turned out of office. England's decisions did not depend on him alone; they were dictated by the consequences of her previous policy and by the fear of an increase of Germany's power. . . .

With France and Russia the case was quite different. I do not doubt that the great body of the people even in these two countries was desirous of peace. In the ruling circles, both in Paris and St. Petersburg, there were two parties; the one wanted peace if it could be maintained consistently with honour, the other wanted war. In France the latter combined with those who cherished the idea of *revanche,* which had never died out. Poincaré and Delcassé were its great protagonists. Since the brush with Germany in Morocco and the founding of the Entente, this party had greatly strengthened its influence; and finally, with Poincaré as leader it had assumed the real management of affairs. In Russia the Czar was the head of the peace party; for a long time the war party was without any real leader. Wide military circles and all those who favoured Pan-Slav ideas supported the war party at St. Petersburg. In Iswolski, after his personal reverse in the Bosnian crisis, they found a zealous champion. As Ambassador in Paris, this vain and vengeful man fell wholly under the sway of the Delcassé and Poincaré group and rendered it the greatest service by his personal influence. His despatches from Paris, the publication of which in a German translation has now been completed, show clearly to anyone who is not blinded by prejudice, by what cautious and subtle methods Iswolski, in conjunction with Poincaré, prepared for the war. He knew how to get rid of refractory elements like Georges Louis, the French Ambassador in St. Petersburg, how to bribe the press and make use of it, and how to exploit the insatiable vanity of Poincaré. It is really difficult to say which of the two led and which followed. There is no doubt as to their close co-operation. Iswolski cannot repeat too often what good luck it is that Poincaré, and not some other less reliable and less skilful politician, stands at the head of France.

So far as guilt can be brought home to individual personalities in the world war, these two men stand convicted. For long years they had prepared the soil by persistent and deliberate effort, always careful not to let their real aims appear, but to wait for the time when the armaments were completed and when one of the opposing Powers, through some indiscretion, offered the possibility of being made to appear the aggressor; for that was necessary not only to win over the opinion of the masses in both countries, but also out of consideration for England, with her cautious Government and peace-loving people. But the aims which these groups pursued could not be achieved without war. The French wished to recover Alsace-Lorraine from the Germans; the Russians wished to open the way to the Straits and to the control of the Balkans, and they wished to free the Slavs from the German, Austrian, and Turkish domination under which they had hitherto lived, and to absorb them within their own sphere of influence. It was they, not Germany, who wished for conquests at the expense of others.

The clever and unscrupulous tunnelling operations of these comparatively small groups prepared the way for the World War. Their leaders were not daunted by the hideous consequences of such a struggle of the nations, for without it they could not reach their goal. They were already waiting their opportunity during the Balkan Wars, and in July, 1914, they seized it gladly. The Russian mobilization, which was the immediate cause of the war, was their work.

Unfortunately we possessed no statesman who was competent to deal with these clever and unscrupulous diplomatists. Austria's rashness and Germany's timid consideration for her last ally gave them the opportunity which they wanted, and they used it with consummate skill.

I have purposely confined myself in all these considerations to the interrelation of the immediate causes of the war, but I cannot close the book without referring briefly to the deeper reasons for this great catastrophe.

The rapid partitioning of Africa and of the South Sea Islands among the European Powers, from about 1880 onwards, created an atmosphere of acute political tension. This was further accentuated after 1895, when it seemed as if the process of dismemberment were to be applied in the Far East and to the territory of Turkey. So long as there was land to dispose of, a policy of compensations served as a safety valve and prevented explosions. But the narrower the available space became, the more stiffly the valve worked and the more it creaked. America's intervention in the Far East and Japan's accession to the dignity of a Great Power, practically closed the whole of eastern Asia against dismemberment for a long time to come. After 1900 the territory of Africa had all been allotted as far as Morocco and Abyssinia. The competition among the Powers was now concentrated on Morocco and the Turkish Empire.

Underlying these international and colonial rivalries lay the powerful economic interests of the leading industrial and commercial nations, each of them anxious to get as large a field as possible for the sale of its goods, and to secure productive sources for the supply of raw materials, and political privileges to ensure remunerative investment for its capital.

Alongside these new international antagonisms there remained the old enmities between the Continental Powers. The greatest of these was the Franco-German rivalry symbolized in Alsace-Lorraine, and the struggle between Austria-Hungary and Russia for the leading position in the Balkans.

Yet underneath these European antagonisms there lay a deeper difficulty. It was the discord which increased throughout the nineteenth century between the State frontiers as settled of old, or as established by treaty, and the principle of nationality, established with such conquering power by the French Revolution. Neither in Eastern Europe, nor in the Balkans, nor between France and Germany, did the boundaries of the States correspond with those of population and language. Austria-Hungary and Turkey were States belonging to an earlier stage of development. They had been created without any regard to the nationality and the wish of the human beings composing them, and they were only maintained with difficulty by the pressure of circumstances. Germany, too, in the north-east, was ruling a large foreign population, and, in 1871, she had absorbed within her empire a French-speaking territory, even if according to its character and to the majority of its inhabitants, it was a national entity in itself.

If the principle of nationality remained the foundation of European States — during these last decades it had grown greatly in strength and significance — these anachronistic States belonging to an earlier generation had to be broken up and removed. Nothing could save them from this fate. When Germany, not realizing this position,

bound up her destiny with that of Austria-Hungary and for a long time supported the effort to maintain and strengthen the Turkish Empire, she committed a gross and disastrous mistake from the point of view of historical development. She linked up her fresh and vigorous national strength with the corrupt remnant of a decaying empire doomed to destruction, and was thereby involved in its ruin. The maintenance of the Danube Monarchy, as a barrier against the flooding of south-eastern Europe by Slav races under Russian leadership, was certainly part of the traditions of the Bismarck School; yet how often Bismarck himself warned us against letting ourselves be pushed into the flames for the expansion of Austria's interests in the Balkans! And that is precisely what happened. . . . By exalting into an inviolable dogma the necessity for the Triple Alliance and for the maintenance of the Danube Monarchy, our statesmen were acting contrary to the spirit of Bismarck and of all sound policy, and robbed themselves of the freedom of movement indispensable for the development of our system of alliances.

Summary Statement of the Revisionist Position

HARRY ELMER BARNES

Like many Americans, Englishmen, and Frenchmen, Professor Barnes became convinced by the early publication of previously secret documents and memoirs that a great injustice had been done to Germany by Article 231 of the Versailles treaty. He left to other historians, however, the task of writing for scholars and sought with noteworthy success to popularize the revisionist position. His presentation, based upon all the available sources, was the most forthright statement made by any student of the subject in the United States. More than any other work, it awakened a reaction in the minds and spirits of Americans to the wartime propaganda of condemnation and hatred of the enemy.

WE HAVE now devoted a series of chapters to the question of war responsibility in each of the major states involved. We may here briefly summarize the general situation in what may be regarded as a brief statement of the revisionist point of view as it appears to the present writer. The general European system after 1870, based as it was upon nationalism, militarism, secret alliances, and imperialistic aims, naturally inclined Europe toward war. The system does not, however, explain why war came in 1914, as the same general European situation had been prevailing for many years prior to that time, though certain problems had become more acute in the years immediately preceding the World War, particularly in the Near East and Morocco.

The Franco-Russian Alliance concluded by 1894 was transformed into an offensive organization following 1912 through the cooperation of Izvolski and Poincaré. Both recognized that the chief objects of Russian and French foreign policy, the seizure of the Straits and the return of Alsace-Lorraine, could be realized only through a general European war. From 1912–14 their joint plans involved a manipulation of the Balkan situation in such a fashion as to be able to take advantage of any crisis likely to provoke a European war, an arrangement to get England so involved that she would be bound to come in on the side of France and Russia, and a great increase in military preparations in France and Russia.

It was decided that Serbia would be the most favorable area in which to create the desired incident in the Balkans. In the early spring of 1914 prominent officers in the Serbian General Staff laid a plot for the assassination of the Archduke, Franz Ferdinand. The Serbian civil government was aware of the plot for at least a month before its execution, but made no adequate effort to stop the plot or to warn Austria. Prominent Russians were also aware of the plot, but the degree of the complicity of Russia is as yet uncertain.

When the assassination came, the French and Russians recognized that the impending clash between Austria and Serbia would constitute a highly appropriate episode over which to bring about the desired conflict. The year 1914 was a particularly desirable year for the Entente because there was imminent danger that England might develop more happy relations with Germany, and that the French Radicals might be able to secure the repeal of the French Army Bill. Poincaré went to St. Petersburg, and, before knowing the terms of the Austrian ultimatum, renewed his pledge of two years earlier to support Russia in a war over the Balkans, and indicated that the probable Austro-Serbian conflict would meet the conditions demanded by the French in supporting Russia in intervention in the Balkans.

The Franco-Russian procedure in 1914 was to indicate a show of conciliation and concessions on the part of Serbia, and apparent Franco-Russian willingness to settle the dispute through diplomacy, while secret Franco-Russian military preparations were to be carried on which would ultimately make a diplomatic settlement quite impossible. Hence, Russia urged Serbia not to declare war on Austria, and, to insure a sufficiently conciliatory Serbian reply to Austria the Serbian response to the Austrian ultimatum was drafted in outline in the French Foreign Office. Russia did not desire to have Serbia precipitate matters prematurely by a declaration of war on Austria, because this would have affected European opinion, particularly English opinion, unfavorably and would also have brought about military activities altogether too rapidly for Russia, whose mobilization over a vast area would necessarily be slow as compared with that of Austria and Germany.

On the 24th of July, the moment Russia and France learned of the terms of the Austrian ultimatum to Serbia, they began that dual program of a diplomatic barrage combined with secret military preparations which had made a European war inevitable by the afternoon of July 30th. Russia sent a diplomatic message to Serbia counselling moderation, but at the same time decided upon the mobilization of the four great military districts of Central and Southern Russia as well as of the Russian fleets. Russian money in Germany and Austria was also called in.

On the same day Viviani telegraphed to the French Foreign Office that the Austro-Serbian situation was likely to develop serious European complications, and the French troops in Morocco were ordered home. Both countries began systematic military preparations for war on the 26th of July. By the 29th the time had come when Russian military preparations had gone far enough to warrant a general mobilization, and the Tsar was persuaded to consent to this order. A telegram from the Kaiser, however, induced him to revoke the order, but the next day Sazonoff and the army officials once more extracted from the Tsar his reluctant consent to the order for general mobilization. The French and the Russians had understood for a generation that once Russian general mobilization was ordered there would be no way of preventing a general European war. General Dobrorolski has told us with great candor that the Russian authorities in 1914 fully realized that a European war was *on* as soon as the mobilization order had been sent out of the general telegraph office in St. Petersburg late in the afternoon of July 30th.

The French authorities had been thoroughly informed as to the nature and progress of the Russian military preparations, but they made no effort to restrain them, though the French well knew that these military activities were bound to render a European war inevitable. They actually urged the Russians to speed up their military preparations, but to be more secretive about them, so as not to alienate England or provoke Germany to counter-mobilization. On the night of July 31st the French government went still further and finally decided for war, handing this information to Izvolski about midnight of the 31st. France was, thus, the first country to declare itself for war in the European crisis of 1914.

The Austrian statesmen in 1914 decided that the time had come when it would be necessary to control the Serbian menace, and they consciously planned an ultimatum to Serbia of such severity that it would be practically impossible for Serbia to concede all of these demands. The plan, then, was to make a show of diplomacy but to move toward certain war. This program was much like that of France and Russia, save for the fact that *Austria desired to provoke nothing but a local punitive war while the plans of France and Russia envisaged a general European conflict.* This is the most important point to be borne in mind when estimating the relative war guilt of Austria as against that of France and Russia.

Germany, formerly friendly to Serbia, was alarmed by the assassination of the Archduke and the resulting menace to her chief ally. Germany therefore agreed to stand behind Austria in the plan of the latter to execute her program of punishing Serbia. The answer of the Serbians to the Austrian ultimatum, however, impressed the Kaiser as satisfactory, and from that time on he was opposed to further military activity on the part of Austria against Serbia.

In cooperation with Sir Edward Grey, Germany began on the 27th of July to urge upon Austria direct negotiations with Russia and the mediation of her dispute with Serbia. Austria at first refused to listen to this advice and declared war upon Serbia on the 28th. Germany then became alarmed at the rumored Russian military preparations and vigorously pressed Austria for a diplomatic settlement of the dispute. Austria did not give way and consent to this until the 31st of July, which was too late to avert a general European war because the Russian mobilization was then in full swing. Germany endeavored without success to secure the suspension of military activities by Russia, and then, after unexpected hesitation and deliberation, declared war upon Russia.

The Russian general mobilization, undertaken with full connivance of the French, was ordered at a time when diplomatic negotiations were moving rapidly toward a satisfactory settlement of the major problems in the crisis. Hence, the Russian general mobilization not only initiated military hostilities, but was also the sole reason for the failure of diplomatic efforts.

England was for peace provided France was not drawn into the conflict, but was determined to come into the War in case France was involved. As France decided from the beginning to stand with Russia for war, and as England refused to attempt to restrain either France or Russia, England was inevitably drawn away from her encouragement of the German efforts towards a diplomatic settlement of the crisis and into the support of the military aggression of France and Russia. She made her decision to enter the War after Germany had proposed to keep out of Belgium and to refrain from attacking France if England would remain neutral. In fact, Germany even suggested that she might guarantee the integrity of France and the French colonies in the event of war if England would promise neutrality. The Belgian issue in England was a pure subterfuge, exploited by Sir Edward Grey to inflame British opinion against Germany and to secure British support of his war policy.

The United States entered the War in part because the British blockade of the ports of the Central Powers led us to have our chief financial stake in the Entente, and partly because of the pro-British sympathies of Ambassador Page and President Wilson, which made it impossible for them to attempt to hold England strictly to international law on the seas. The English violations of international law in regard to neutral rights provoked the German submarine warfare in retaliation. This submarine warfare furnished the ostensible excuse for the American entry into the conflict. Yet, nearly a year before the resumption of submarine warfare, Mr. Wilson had secretly conveyed to England his intention to enter the war on the side of the Entente if Germany would not accept terms of peace which only a conquered state could have been expected to concede.

In estimating the order of guilt of the various countries we may safely say that the only direct and immediate responsibility for the World War falls upon Serbia, France and Russia, with the guilt about equally distributed. Next in order — far below France and Russia — would come Austria, though she never desired a general European war. Finally, we should place Germany and England as tied for last place, both being opposed to war in the 1914 crisis. Probably the German public was somewhat more favorable to military activities than the English people, but, as we have amply explained above, the Kaiser made much more strenuous efforts to preserve the peace of Europe in 1914 than did Sir Edward Grey.

Origins of the World War

SIDNEY BRADSHAW FAY

While the revisionist battle was raging on all fronts, from the daily press to scholarly conferences and journals, and new revelations were ever bursting into print to furnish fresh ammunition for both sides, Professor Fay set to work quietly and systematically to rewrite the diplomatic backgrounds of the war and to unravel the tangled story of the 1914 crisis. His *Origins of the World War*, which appeared in 1928, was the first major work by an American historian to attempt a sober analysis of the whole problem, and immediately put him in the front ranks of the moderate revisionists who were now more concerned with critical judgment than with polemical acumen. His conclusions, reprinted below, have stood the test of time remarkably well, despite the additional sources and the changes in emphasis that have occurred since 1928.

NONE OF THE Powers wanted a European War. Their governing rulers and ministers, with very few exceptions, all foresaw that it must be a frightful struggle, in which the political results were not absolutely certain, but in which the loss of life, suffering, and economic consequences were bound to be terrible. This is true, in a greater or less degree, of Pashitch, Berchtold, Bethmann, Sazonoff, Poincaré, San Giuliano and Sir Edward Grey. Yet none of them, not even Sir Edward Grey, could have foreseen that the political results were to be so stupendous, and the other consequences so terrible, as was actually the case.

For many of the Powers, to be sure, a European War might seem to hold out the possibility of achieving various desired advantages: for Serbia, the achievement of national unity for all Serbs; for Austria, the revival of her waning prestige as a Great Power, and the checking of nationalistic tendencies which threatened her very existence; for Russia, the accomplishment of her historic mission of controlling Constantinople and the Straits; for Germany, new economic advantages and the restoration of the European balance which had changed with the weakening of the Triple Alliance and the tightening of the Triple Entente; for France, the recovery of Alsace-Lorraine and the ending of the German menace; and for England, the destruction of the German naval danger and of Prussian militarism. All these advantages, and many others, were feverishly striven and intrigued for, on all sides, the moment the War actually broke out, but this is no good proof that any of the statesmen mentioned deliberately aimed to bring about a war to secure these advantages. One cannot judge the motives which actuated men before the War, by what they did in an absolutely new situation which arose as soon as they were overtaken by a conflagration they had sought to avert. And in fact, in the case of the two Powers between whom the immediate conflict arose, the postponement or avoidance of a European War would have facilitated the accomplishment of the ultimate advantages aimed at:

Pashitch knew that there was a better chance for Serbian national unity after he had consolidated Serbian gains in the Balkan Wars, and after Russia had completed her military and naval armaments as planned for 1917; and Berchtold knew that he had a better chance of crushing the Greater Serbia danger and strengthening Austria, if he could avoid Russian intervention and a general European War. . . .

Nevertheless, a European War broke out. Why? Because in each country political and military leaders did certain things which led to mobilizations and declarations of war, or failed to do certain things which might have prevented them. In this sense, all the European countries, in a greater or less degree, were responsible. One must abandon the dictum of the Versailles Treaty that Germany and her allies were solely responsible. It was a dictum exacted by victors from vanquished, under the influence of the blindness, ignorance, hatred, and the propagandist misconceptions to which war had given rise. It was based on evidence which was incomplete and not always sound.[1] It is generally recognized by the best historical scholars in all countries to be no longer tenable or defensible. They are agreed that the responsibility for the War is a divided responsibility. But they still disagree very much as to the relative part of this responsibility that falls on each country and on each individual political or military leader.

Some writers like to fix positively in some precise mathematical fashion the exact responsibility for the war. This was done in one way by the framers of Article 231 of the Treaty of Versailles. It has been done in other ways by those who would fix the responsibility in some relative fashion, as, for instance, Austria first, then Russia, France and Germany and England. But the present writer deprecates such efforts to assess by a precise formula a very complicated question, which is after all more a matter of delicate shading than of definite white and black. Oversimplification, as Napoleon once said in framing his Code, is the enemy of precision. Moreover, even supposing that a general consensus of opinion might be reached as to the relative responsibility of any individual country or man for immediate causes connected with the July crisis of 1914, it is by no means necessarily true that the same relative responsibility would hold for the underlying causes, which for years had been tending toward the creation of a dangerous situation.

One may, however, sum up very briefly the most salient facts in regard to each country.

Serbia felt a natural and justifiable impulse to do what so many other countries had done in the nineteenth century — to bring under one national Government all the discontented Serb people. She had liberated those under Turkish rule; the next step was to liberate those under Hapsburg rule. She looked to Russia for assistance, and had been encouraged to expect that she would receive it. After the assassination, Mr. Pashitch took no steps to discover and bring to justice Serbians in Belgrade who had been implicated in the plot. One of them, Ciganovitch, was even assisted to disappear. Mr. Pashitch waited to see what evidence the Austrian authorities could find. When Austria demanded cooperation of Austrian officials in discovering, though not in trying, implicated Serbians, the Serbian Government made a very conciliatory but negative reply. They expected that the reply would not be regarded as satisfactory, and, even before it was given, ordered the mobilization of the Serbian army. Serbia did not want war, but believed it would be forced upon her. That Mr. Pashitch was aware of the plot three weeks before it was executed, failed to take effective steps to prevent the assassins from

[1] For a recent analysis of the evidence laid before the Commission on Responsibility for the War at the Paris Peace Conference, and the untenability of the conclusions based upon it, see A. von Wegerer, "Die Wiederlegung der Versailles Kriegsschuldthese," in *Die Kriegsschuldfrage*, VI, 1–77, Jan., 1928; also his article, with replies to it, in *Current History*, Aug., 1928, pp. 810–828.

crossing over from Serbia to Bosnia, and then failed to give Austria any warning or information which might have averted the fatal crime, were facts unknown to Austria in July, 1914; they cannot therefore be regarded as in any way justifying Austria's conduct; but they are part of Serbia's responsibility, and a very serious part.

Austria was more responsible for the immediate origin of the war than any other Power. Yet from her own point of view she was acting in self-defence — not against an immediate military attack, but against the corroding Greater Serbia and Jugoslav agitation which her leaders believed threatened her very existence. No State can be expected to sit with folded arms and await dismemberment at the hands of its neighbors. Russia was believed to be intriguing with Serbia and Rumania against the Dual Monarchy. The assassination of the heir to the throne, as a result of a plot prepared in Belgrade, demanded severe retribution; otherwise Austria would be regarded as incapable of action, "wormeaten" as the Serbian Press expressed it, would sink in prestige, and hasten her own downfall. To avert this Berchtold determined to crush Serbia with war. He deliberately framed the ultimatum with the expectation and hope that it would be rejected. He hurriedly declared war against Serbia in order to forestall all efforts at mediation. He refused even to answer his own ally's urgent requests to come to an understanding with Russia, on the basis of a military occupation of Belgrade as a pledge that Serbia would carry out the promises in her reply to the ultimatum. Berchtold gambled on a "local" war with Serbia only, believing that he could rattle the German sword; but rather than abandon his war with Serbia, he was ready to drag the rest of Europe into war.

It is very questionable whether Berchtold's obstinate determination to diminish Serbia and destroy her as a Balkan factor was, after all, the right method, even if he had succeeded in keeping the war "localized" and in temporarily strengthening the Dual Monarchy. Supposing that Russia in

1914, because of military unpreparedness or lack of support, had been ready to tolerate the execution of Berchtold's designs, it is quite certain that she would have aimed within the next two or three years at wiping out this second humiliation, which was so much more damaging to her prestige than that of 1908–09. In two or three years, when her great program of military reform was finally completed, Russia would certainly have found a pretext to reverse the balance in the Balkans in her own favor again. A further consequence of Berchtold's policy, even if successful, would have been the still closer consolidation of the Triple Entente, with the possible addition of Italy. And, finally, a partially dismembered Serbia would have become a still greater source of unrest and danger to the peace of Europe than heretofore. Serbian nationalism, like Polish nationalism, would have been intensified by partition. Austrian power and prestige would not have been so greatly increased as to be able to meet these new dangers. Berchtold's plan was a mere temporary improvement, but could not be a final solution of the Austro-Serbian antagonism. Franz Ferdinand and many others recognized this, and so long as he lived, no step in this fatal direction had been taken. It was the tragic fate of Austria that the only man who might have had the power and ability to develop Austria along sound lines became the innocent victim of the crime which was the occasion of the World War and so of her ultimate disruption.

Germany did not plot a European War, did not want one, and made genuine, though too belated efforts, to avert one. She was the victim of her alliance with Austria and of her own folly. Austria was her only dependable ally, Italy and Rumania having become nothing but allies in name. She could not throw her over, as otherwise she would stand isolated between Russia, where Panslavism and armaments were growing stronger every year, and France, where Alsace-Lorraine, Delcassé's fall, and Agadir were not forgotten. Therefore, Bethmann felt bound to accede to

Berchtold's request for support and gave him a free hand to deal with Serbia; he also hoped and expected to "localize" the Austro-Serbian conflict. Germany then gave grounds to the Entente for suspecting the sincerity of her peaceful intentions by her denial of any foreknowledge of the ultimatum, by her support and justification of it when it was published, and by her refusal of Sir Edward Grey's conference proposal. However, Germany by no means had Austria so completely under her thumb as the Entente Powers and many writers have assumed. It is true that Berchtold would hardly have embarked on his gambler's policy unless he had been assured that Germany would fulfil the obligations of the alliance, and to this extent Germany must share the great responsibility of Austria. But when Bethmann realized that Russia was likely to intervene, that England might not remain neutral, and that there was danger of a world war of which Germany and Austria would appear to be the instigators, he tried to call a halt on Austria, but it was too late. He pressed mediation proposals on Vienna, but Berchtold was insensible to the pressure, and the Entente Powers did not believe in the sincerity of his pressure, especially as they produced no results.

Germany's geographical position between France and Russia, and her inferiority in number of troops, had made necessary the plan of crushing the French army quickly at first and then turning against Russia. This was only possible, in the opinion of her strategists, by marching through Belgium, as it was generally anticipated by military men that she would do in case of a European War. On July 29, after Austria had declared war on Serbia, and after the Tsar had assented to general mobilization in Russia (though this was not known in Berlin and was later postponed for a day owing to the Kaiser's telegram to the Tsar), Bethmann took the precaution of sending to the German Minister in Brussels a sealed envelope. The Minister was not to open it except on further instructions. It contained the later demand for the passage of the German army through Belgium. This does not mean, however, that Germany had decided for war. In fact, Bethmann was one of the last of the statesmen to abandon hope of peace and to consent to the mobilization of his country's army. General mobilization of the continental armies took place in the following order: Serbia, Russia, Austria, France and Germany. General mobilization by a Great Power was commonly interpreted by military men in every country, though perhaps not by Sir Edward Grey, the Tsar, and some civilian officials. as meaning that the country was on the point of making war, — that the military machine had begun to move and would not be stopped. Hence, when Germany learned of the Russian general mobilization, she sent ultimatums to St. Petersburg and Paris, warning that German mobilization would follow unless Russia suspended hers within twelve hours, and asking what would be the attitude of France. The answers being unsatisfactory, Germany then mobilized and declared war. It was the hasty Russian general mobilization, assented to on July 29 and ordered on July 30, while Germany was still trying to bring Austria to accept mediation proposals, which finally rendered the European War inevitable.

Russia was partly responsible for the Austro-Serbian conflict because of the frequent encouragement which she had given at Belgrade — that Serbian national unity would be ultimately achieved with Russian assistance at Austrian expense. This had led the Belgrade Cabinet to hope for Russian support in case of a war with Austria, and the hope did not prove vain in July, 1914. Before this, to be sure, in the Bosnian Crisis and during the Balkan Wars, Russia had put restraint upon Serbia, because Russia, exhausted by the effects of the Russo-Japanese War, was not yet ready for a European struggle with the Teutonic Powers. But in 1914 her armaments, though not yet completed, had made such progress that the militarists were confident of success, if they had French and British support. In the spring of 1914, the Minister of War, Sukhomlinov, had published an article in a Russian newspaper, though without signing his name, to the effect, "Russia is ready, France must be ready also." Austria was convinced that Russia would ultimately aid Serbia, unless the Serbian danger were dealt with energetically after the Archduke's murder; she knew that Russia was growing stronger every year; but she doubted whether the Tsar's armaments had yet reached the point at which Russia would dare to intervene; she would therefore run less risk of Russian intervention and a European War if she used the Archduke's assassination as an excuse for weakening Serbia, than if she should postpone action until the future.

Russia's responsibility lay also in the secret preparatory military measures which she was making at the same time that she was carrying on diplomatic negotiations. These alarmed Germany and Austria. But it was primarily Russia's general mobilization, made when Germany was trying to bring Austria to a settlement, which precipitated the final catastrophe, causing Germany to mobilize and declare war.

The part of France is less clear than that of the other Great Powers, because she has not yet made a full publication of her documents. To be sure, M. Poincaré, in the fourth volume of his memoirs, has made a skilful and elaborate plea, to prove *La France innocente*. But he is not convincing. It is quite clear that on his visit to Russia he assured the Tsar's Government that France would support her as an ally in preventing Austria from humiliating or crushing Serbia. Paléologue renewed these assurances in a way to encourage Russia to take a strong hand. He did not attempt to restrain Russia from military measures which he knew would call forth German counter-measures and cause war. Nor did he keep his Government promptly and fully informed of the military steps which were being taken at St. Petersburg. President Poincaré, upon his return to France, made efforts for peace, but his great preoccupation was to minimize French and Russian preparatory measures and emphasize those of Germany, in order to secure the certainty of British support in a struggle which he now regarded as inevitable.

Sir Edward Grey made many sincere proposals for preserving peace; they all failed owing partly, but not exclusively, to Germany's attitude. Sir Edward could probably have prevented war if he had done either of two things. If, early in the crisis, he had acceded to the urging of France and Russia and given a strong warning to Germany that, in a European War, England would take the side of the Franco-Russian Alliance, this would probably have led Bethmann to exert an earlier and more effective pressure on Austria; and it would perhaps thereby have prevented the Austrian declaration of war on Serbia, and brought to a successful issue the "direct conversations" between Vienna and St. Petersburg. Or, if Sir Edward Grey had listened to German urging, and warned France and Russia early in the crisis, that if they became involved in war, England would remain neutral, probably Russia would have hesitated with her mobilizations, and France would probably have exerted a restraining influence at St. Petersburg. But Sir Edward Grey could not say that England would take the side of France and Russia, because he had a Cabinet nearly evenly divided, and he was not sure, early in the crisis, that public opinion in England would back him up in war against Germany. He could resign, and he says in his memoirs that he would have resigned, but that would have been no comfort or aid to France, who had come confidently to count upon British support. He was determined to say and do nothing which might encourage her with a hope which he could not fulfil. Therefore, in spite of the pleadings of the French, he refused to give them definite assurances until the probable German determination to go through Belgium made it clear that the Cabinet, and Parliament, and British public opinion would follow his lead in war on Germany.

On the other hand, he was unwilling to heed the German pleadings that he exercise restraint at Paris and St. Petersburg, because he did not wish to endanger the Anglo-Russian Entente and the solidarity of the Triple Entente, because he felt a moral obligation to France, growing out of the Anglo-French military and naval conversations of the past years, and because he suspected that Germany was backing Austria up in an unjustifiable course and that Prussian militarists had taken the direction of affairs at Berlin out of the hands of Herr von Bethmann-Hollweg and the civilian authorities.

Italy exerted relatively little influence on the crisis in either direction.

Belgium had done nothing in any way to justify the demand which Germany made upon her. With commendable prudence, at the very first news of the ominous Austrian ultimatum, she had foreseen the danger to which she might be exposed. She had accordingly instructed her representatives abroad as to the statements which they were to make in case Belgium should decide very suddenly to mobilize to protect her neutrality. On July 29, she placed her army upon "a strengthened war footing," but did not order complete mobilization until two days later, when Austria, Russia, and Germany had already done so, and war appeared inevitable. Even after being confronted with the terrible German ultimatum, at 7 P.M. on August 2, she did not at once invite the assistance of English and French troops to aid her in the defense of her soil and her neutrality against a certain German assault; it was not until German troops had actually violated her territory,

on August 4, that she appealed for the assistance of the Powers which had guaranteed her neutrality. Belgium was the innocent victim of German strategic necessity. Though the German violation of Belgium was of enormous influence in forming public opinion as to the responsibility for the War after hostilities began, it was not a cause of the War, except in so far as it made it easier for Sir Edward Grey to bring England into it.

In the forty years following the Franco-Prussian War, as we have seen, there developed a system of alliances which divided Europe into two hostile groups. This hostility was accentuated by the increase of armaments, economic rivalry, nationalist ambitions and antagonisms, and newspaper incitement. But it is very doubtful whether all these dangerous tendencies would have actually led to war, had it not been for the assassination of Franz Ferdinand. That was the factor which consolidated the elements of hostility and started the rapid and complicated succession of events which culminated in a World War, and for that factor Serbian nationalism was primarily responsible.

But the verdict of the Versailles Treaty that Germany and her allies were responsible for the War, in view of the evidence now available, is historically unsound. It should therefore be revised. However, because of the popular feeling widespread in some of the Entente countries, it is doubtful whether a formal and legal revision is as yet practicable. There must first come a further revision by historical scholars, and through them of public opinion.

II. WHY THE WAR IN 1914?

The Coming of the War

GEORGE PEABODY GOOCH

The dean of British historians early took an interest in the origins of the First World War, but in his published books he has not entered the war guilt fray. His *History of Modern Europe, 1878–1919* (New York, 1923), exclusively devoted to international relations, was for many years the best available text on the period, but told the story as Gooch saw it without reference to the current controversy. With Harold Temperley, he supervised the selection and editing of the *British Documents on the Origins of the War, 1898–1914* (London, 1926–38, 11 v.). His books and articles have placed him in the camp of the revisionists, but his critical approach to his subject has marked him always as a thorough and unusually objective scholar rather than a special pleader. In his *Before the War* he has chosen to study the policies of each of the Great-Power foreign ministers, instead of presenting an exposition of international relations from 1902 to 1914. The first excerpt below is taken from his chapter on Poincaré. The second is the editor's rearrangement of material in Gooch's three separate chapters on Berchtold of Austria-Hungary, Bethmann-Hollweg of Germany, and Sazonov of Russia. This reorganization provides a chronologically continuous story of the July crisis and the fullest account to be included in these readings.

I

POINCARÉ'S stature was recognised in every quarter. He was never beloved, but the semi-official *Norddeutsche Allgemeine Zeitung* rightly saluted him as *l'homme de confiance* of the French people.[1] "From the beginning of his Ministry he has been the living expression of a great patriotic activity in the internal and external policy of his country. In the Eastern crisis he has put his talents at the service of European peace." In none of the extracts from the German press sent home by Jules Cambon is there a hint that he was regarded beyond the Rhine as a warmonger or an enemy. The despatches of the Austrian

Ambassador depict a statesman Russophil indeed, but far more moderate than Iswolsky.[2] There is not a word in the five massive volumes of the *Documents diplomatiques français* covering his year at the Quai d'Orsay to suggest that he desired or worked for war. Not till the publication of selections from Iswolsky's despatches in *Un Livre Noir** in 1922 did the notion arise that in the closing months of 1912 he was recklessly playing with fire by giving Russia a free hand and indeed egging her on.

[1] D.D.F. V, 294–6. [*Documents diplomatiques français,* 3rd series (Paris, 1929–36), 11 v.]

[2] A. IV, 745–6, 814–6, etc. [Austria: *Österreich-Ungarns Aussenpolitik . . . 1908–1914* (Vienna and Leipzig, 1930), 8 v.]

* A collection of Russian documents, translated by René Marchand from Soviet publications (2 v., Paris, 1922–23). [Editor's Note.]

From G. P. Gooch, *Before the War,* II. *The Coming of the War* (London, New York, and Toronto, 1938), pp. 197–99, 269–86, 364–70, and 439–47. Reprinted by permission of G. P. Gooch.

Poincaré's reply is that the Russian Ambassador, whom he distrusted and disliked, is a thoroughly unreliable witness.[3] "In this jumble of documents published by the Bolshevists," he writes in his *Souvenirs,* "one can discover a few passages which, carefully separated from the context, are capable of different interpretations. But, as M. Herriot said in the Chamber of Deputies on July 6, 1922, if one studies the *Livre Noir* page by page, one finds nothing to compromise the Government of the Republic. . . . I knew that personal preoccupations played a capital part in his policy. "Il ne se gênait pas pour substituer ses idées à celles de son gouvernement. Il traduisait à sa manière les instructions qu'il recevait et les réponses qui lui étaient faites au Quai d'Orsay. . . . Suivant une méthode chère à quelques représentants étrangers, il prêtait volontiers à ses interlocuteurs, dans sa correspondance officielle, le langage qu'il avait intérêt à leur faire tenir ou les conceptions qu'il voulait suggérer à son gouvernement, sans en prendre lui-même la responsabilité." ["He felt no constraint at substituting his own ideas for those of his government. He interpreted in his own way the instructions which he received and the replies which were made to him by the Quai d'Orsay. . . . Following a procedure favored by some foreign representatives, he, of his own volition, in his official correspondence attributed to those who talked with him the language which it was to his interest to have them use or the ideas which he wished to suggest to his own government without having to take responsibility for them."]

Could Iswolsky have rebutted these grave accusations had he lived to read them? Probably not, though he would certainly have denied them. Not all diplomatists are equally accurate or conscientious reporters of conversations in which the turn of a phrase, the omission of a qualification, or the suppression of a point may make all the difference. Whatever may be thought of Poincaré's policy in 1912 or afterwards, his character stands higher than that of the Russian Ambassador. "I declare on my honour," he wrote shortly before his death, "that I never said a word to him which allowed him to expect from me an extension of the Franco-Russian alliance."[4] Iswolsky's correspondence is an insufficient foundation for the graver charges levelled against him by critics at home and abroad. We approach nearest to the truth if we conclude that, like the ardent patriot he was, he put new vigour into French policy, and that, like a good lawyer, he operated the Russian alliance without straying beyond the letter of its obligations.

Yet the Russian Ambassador was correct in sensing an atmospheric change. Poincaré's accession to office, writes the most impartial and authoritative of French historians, opened a new phase, in which the French Government felt the need to revive the intimacy of the alliance.[5] The experience of the Agadir crisis had shown what a bitter memory Russian statesmen retained of the attitude of France in the Bosnian crisis. If fresh Franco-German difficulties arose, was it not essential to count on stronger Russian support? And if reciprocity was to be assured, was it not necessary to manifest a greater interest in Russia's Balkan policy? That was the probable explanation of the new tendencies revealed in the application of the alliance in November 1912, when Poincaré, in view of a possible Austro-Russian conflict about a Serb port, adopted a more decided attitude. Of course he was very careful to say that the military support of France was limited to the *casus foederis,* that is to the hypothesis that Germany intervened to support Austria against Russia. But, unlike Pichon, he

---

[3] [Raymond Poincaré, *Au Service de la France: neuf années de souvenirs* (Paris, 1926–33), 10 v. Cited as] *Souvenirs,* I, ch. 10, and [René Gerin and Raymond Poincaré] *Les Responsabilités de la guerre* [Paris, 1930], 47–67.

[4] *Les Responsabilités de la guerre,* 51.

[5] Renouvin, *Les Engagements de l'Alliance Franco-Russe,* in *Revue d'histoire de la Guerre Mondiale,* October 1934.

admitted the eventuality of a general war about Balkan questions.

In a word, under the stress of events, a broader interpretation of the partnership was advanced. The probability of a general conflict grew with the Agadir crisis and increased still further with the Balkan struggle. The Grey-Cambon letters offered no such support as the logical French mind, which craves for precision, hungered to receive. Russia alone could be counted on in case of need, just as Germany and Austria formed an indivisible *bloc*. Bethmann's historic speech in the Reichstag on December 2, 1912, breathed the same message of unflinching solidarity as Poincaré's conversations with Iswolsky. Neither statesman had the slightest desire for a major conflagration, the result of which was unpredictable. Yet both were ready to fight for the Balance of Power, that master principle which inspired treaties, cemented ententes, and guided the Chancelleries of Europe on their perilous course.

II*

The Kaiser's first instinct on hearing the news of the Serajevo murders was to hurry to Vienna, but he was dissuaded by Bethmann on the ground of danger to life.[1] To a telegram regretting inability to express his sympathy in person Francis Joseph replied in an autograph letter which was brought by Count Hoyos to Berlin on July 5, together with a Foreign Office Memorandum setting forth the case for action against Serbia and advocating an alliance with Bulgaria. He had expected strong action, remarked the Kaiser, but as European complications had to be considered he could give no formal answer till he had consulted the Chancellor. After lunch he authorised the Ambassador to inform his master that

he could rely on Germany's full support.[2] As he had said, he must first ascertain the Chancellor's view, but he felt certain that the latter would agree. Even if it came to war between Austria and Russia, the former could be sure that Germany with her usual loyalty would stand at her side. Russia, however, was by no means ready and would think twice before appealing to arms. He realised how hard it would be for the peace-loving Emperor to march into Serbia, but, if it were deemed necessary, he would regret the loss of a favourable opportunity. Later in the afternoon he received the Chancellor and the Under-Secretary Zimmermann, as Jagow was on leave. The preservation of Austria, he declared, was a vital interest of Germany. It was not their task to advise a course of action, but Francis Joseph should be assured that Germany would stand at Austria's side. Bethmann expressed his assent.

On the following day the Austrian Ambassador conversed with the Chancellor and Zimmermann.[3] His master, began Bethmann, had instructed him to express gratitude for the autograph letter. The German Government recognised the dangers arising from Russia's plans of a Balkan League. They also understood why Austria desired the adhesion of Bulgaria to the Triple Alliance, though they hoped that it would not weaken the obligations to Rumania. The German Minister in Sofia would, if desired, negotiate with the Bulgarian Government. King Carol would be informed of the negotiations in Sofia, and would be urged to suppress the Austrophobe agitation in his country. As regards Austria's relations with Serbia, it was for her to decide what must be done. Whatever her decision, she could be sure that Germany would stand at her side as ally and friend. The Chancellor, like his master, reported Szogenyi, regarded immediate action as the best solution of Austria's

* [This section has been rearranged to make a continuous narrative—ED.]

[1] *Die deutschen Dokumente zum Kriegsausbruch*, ed. Kautsky, are supplemented by Dirr, *Bayerische Dokumente*, and Bach, *Deutsche Gesandtschaftsberichte zum Kriegsausbruch*. The fullest account from the German side is by Hermann Lutz, *Die Europäische Politik in der Julikrise, 1914*, published in 1930.

[2] A. VIII, 306–7, 319–20. [Austria: *Österreich-Ungarns Aussenpolitik . . . 1908–1914* (Vienna and Leipzig, 1930), 8 v.]
[3] *Ibid.*

difficulties in the Balkans, and from an international standpoint he considered the present moment more favourable than later. He approved the concealment of the plan from Italy and Rumania. On the other hand Italy should be informed of the intention of her allies to bring Bulgaria into the Triple Alliance. Thus, though neither Kaiser nor Chancellor had the slightest desire for a European war, they encouraged Austria to go ahead.

As Bethmann explains in his apologia, if Austria collapsed or changed sides, exasperated by being left in the lurch on a vital issue, Germany would find herself alone. That they should reject the appeal was indeed unthinkable. The mistake was to give Berchtold a free hand. Vienna, he declares, would have disliked interference, and diplomatic co-operation would have prevented Germany playing her mediator's part. He denies having given a blank cheque, since he asked to be kept informed and learned the outlines of the coming demands through his Ambassador. Yet he confesses that he considered the ultimatum too sharp, and it was precisely on the contents of that document that the destiny of the world was to turn. Jagow equally denies that Austria was given *carte blanche*; but he too was surprised by the sharp tone, and complained when the Austrian Ambassador declared that it was too late to change.[4] Whatever the intention of Berlin, Berchtold believed he was given a free hand and went his way.

. . . . . .

When the Austrian torpedo was about to be launched the Chancellor sent a circular despatch dated July 21 to the Ambassadors in St. Petersburg, Paris and London, recalling Pan-Serb provocations and Austria's magnanimity. She could no longer watch unmoved the threats to her security and integrity. Her demands, though fair and moderate, might have to be enforced. The Ambassadors were instructed to explain the German view that it was a question solely affecting Austria and Serbia. "We ardently desire the localisation of the conflict, since, in view of the various alliances, any intervention by another Power would involve unpredictable consequences." A special message accompanied the despatch to St. Petersburg. "You will also call the attention of Sazonoff to the grave consequences to the monarchical idea if the monarchical Powers, putting aside their national sympathies and political points of view, do not stand squarely at the side of Austria. For the political radicalism which rules in Serbia, and which does not stop short of crimes against its own royal family, must be crushed. In this task Russia is as much interested as Germany."

. . . . . .

The ultimatum presented at Belgrad by Giesl, the Austrian Minister, at 6 P.M. on July 23 began by recalling the promise of neighbourly relations made on March 31, 1909, and contrasting it with the record of the following years.[5] The events of June 28 had proclaimed the fatal results of tolerating criminal activities. The murder had been plotted in Belgrad; the weapons and explosives had been supplied by Serb officers and officials belonging to the Narodna Obrana; and the entry into Bosnia had been arranged by frontier officials. The Imperial Government must put an end to the machinations which constituted a chronic menace to the tranquillity of the Monarchy. It was therefore compelled to ask for an official condemnation of the hostile propaganda which aimed at detaching portions of Austrian territory, and the suppression of criminal and terrorist activities. Ten demands followed — control of publications, dissolution of the Narodna Obrana, supervision of education, dismissal of Austrophobe officers and officials, collaboration in the suppression of the movement against

[4] Jagow, *Ursachen und Ausbruch des Weltkrieges* [Berlin, 1919], 110.

[5] A. VIII, 515–17. The critical days in Belgrad are described in Giesl, *Zwei Jahrzehnte im Nahen Orient* [Berlin, 1927], ch. 12, and Loncarevich, *Jugoslaviens Entstehung* [Vienna, 1928], 589–623.

the territorial integrity of the Monarchy, a judicial examination of the accomplices of the Serajevo plot (in which Austrian representatives would take part), arrest of two Serbs implicated in the murders, prevention of the passage of munitions across the frontier, explanations of hostile utterances by high officials after the murders, and a speedy report on the execution of the demands. A reply was requested within forty-eight hours. There was not an accusation in it, declared Berchtold many years later, which could not be proved, nor a demand which could not be justified by the facts in Austria's possession.[6] Musulin, who drafted it, testifies that the Foreign Office believed that Serbia would accept, but Giesl did not.[7]

The second act of the drama opened on the evening of July 23, when the Russian Chargé in Belgrad wired that a forty-eight hours' ultimatum had been presented at 6 P.M. The Finance Minister, he added, who represented Pashitch in his absence, begged for the help of Russia, and declared that no Serbian Government could accept the demands. A second telegram summarised the contents. When Sazonoff reached the Foreign Office on the morning of July 24 and heard the news from Schilling, he exclaimed: *C'est la guerre européenne.* He telephoned to the Tsar, who exclaimed: It is monstrous. At this moment the Austrian Ambassador brought the full text, which prompted Sazonoff to exclaim: "You are setting Europe alight. You have burned your bridges."[8] Sazonoff lunched with Paléologue to meet Buchanan, and the Rumanian Minister arrived later. To the Governments which they represented he conveyed a pressing request to discuss common action, adding that the neutrality of England would mean suicide. A Council of Ministers was held in the afternoon, at which he reported the presen-

tation of unacceptable demands at Belgrad and Serbia's request for help. Five conclusions were reached. The first approved his proposal to secure an extension of the time limit. The second approved his suggested advice to Serbia not to resist invasion if she was too weak, but to entrust her fate to the Powers. The third advised the mobilisation of the military districts of Kieff, Odessa, Moscow and Kazan, and of the Baltic and Black Sea fleets, in case of need. The fourth urged the replenishment of army supplies, the fifth the recall of money lying in German and Austrian banks. After the Council the Foreign Minister saw the Serbian Minister and advised the utmost moderation in replying to the Austrian note. During the evening the German Ambassador endeavoured to justify the action of Austria and emphasised the importance of "the monarchical principle." Sazonoff sharply condemned the methods of the Austrian Government, declared the note unacceptable by Serbia, and complained that the short time-limit gave the Powers no chance to examine the situation.

In Sazonoff's opinion the best, if not the only, hope of averting war was for England to speak. What he had in mind was another "Mansion House speech." It was easier for her, he telegraphed to London on July 25, to moderate Austria, for in Vienna she was regarded as the most impartial Power. Since the Ballplatz evidently counted on her neutrality, England should declare that she disapproved this dangerous policy. "In the event of the worsening of the situation, which may involve action by the Great Powers, we assume that England will not hesitate to take her stand at the side of Russia and France in order to maintain the balance of power as she has always done." On the same day he suggested that Serbia should ask England to mediate, since her impartiality was above suspicion. He also appealed to Italy to inform Austria of her disapproval of a conflict which could not be localised.

.   .   .   .   .   .

The reception of the ultimatum in

6 [Eduard Ritter von Steinitz,] *Rings um Sazonoff* [Berlin, 1928], 50.

7 Musulin, *Das Haus am Ballplatz* [Murich, 1924], 219–30.

8 A. VIII, 645–8.

Europe was precisely what might have been expected. Grey described it as the most formidable document ever presented to an independent state. "We may have a European war in a week," remarked King Carol. . . . The Serbian reply denied the charge of hostility to Austria, and disclaimed responsibility for the utterances of the press and private societies.[9] Most of the ten demands, including the dissolution of the Narodna Obrana, were accepted. The vital article on Austrian collaboration was accepted within the limits of international law, criminal procedure, and neighbourly relations. If the Austrian Government were not satisfied with the response, the Serbian Government was prepared to submit the question to the decision of the Hague Court or the Great Powers. Unconditional acceptance having been refused, the Austrian Minister promptly left Belgrad on the evening of July 25. On the same day an elaborate *dossier* was despatched to the capitals of Europe setting forth the grounds for the charge of systematic hostility to Austria and of responsibility for the murders of June 28.[10]

Whether or not the Austro-Serb conflict would be localised depended on Russia, and to Russia Berchtold now turned.[11] "In resolving to deal firmly with Serbia," began the instructions to his Ambassador dated July 25, "we are of course aware of the possibility of a collision with Russia. We could not, however, allow this eventuality to divert us, since fundamental considerations of state compel us to terminate a situation in which Russian patronage renders possible the chronic menacing of the Monarchy. If Russia feels that the moment has come for the great reckoning with the Central Powers, these instructions are naturally superfluous." Perhaps, however, she was not so bellicose as her press and perchance Poincaré and Iswolsky might desire. Austria, it should be pointed out, was

territorially satisfied. "If the struggle with Serbia is forced upon us, it will not be for territorial gain but simply a means of self-defence and self-preservation."

In calling attention to the *dossier* the Ambassador was instructed to remind Sazonoff that never had a Great Power borne the disruptive intrigues of a little neighbour with such patience. While Serbia had faced her old Turkish enemy, Austria had held her hand. Now that her aspirations in Turkey were realized and the subversive movement threatened the Monarchy, the situation had changed. "We must assume that conservative and dynastic Russia will understand and indeed approve our action against the menace to the tranquillity of the state." There was no thought of an attack on Orthodox Slavdom, for relations with Montenegro were excellent. Austria wished neither to obtain territory nor to infringe Serbian sovereignty. She was, however, determined to enforce her demands, and she would not shrink from the possibility of European complications. "We should regret a breach of European peace all the more because we have always felt that the partitioning of the Turkish heritage and the growth of strong and independent Balkan states had removed all danger of antagonism between ourselves and Russia. We were ever ready to consider her large political interests, and we always hoped that the similar conservative, monarchical and dynastic interests of the three Empires would improve our relations. Further toleration of Serbian intrigues would have undermined our existence as a state and our position as a Great Power, and thereby jeopardised the European equilibrium. . . . Our action against Serbia, whatever form it assumes, is thoroughly conservative, and its object is the preservation of our position in Europe." To the Russian Ambassador Berchtold repeatedly explained that Austria had no quarrel with Russia.[12]

[9] A. VIII, 660–3.
[10] A. VIII, 665–704.
[11] A. VIII, 721–4.

[12] *Imperialismus*, V, 208–9, 262. [*Die Internationalen Beziehungen im Zeitalter des Imperialismus*, Series I (Berlin, 1931 ff.) — A German translation of a Russian publication of documents.]

Such arguments and declarations, however convincing they sounded at Vienna, fell flat at St. Petersburg, where Russia's historic rôle as the champion of the Balkan Slavs was the paramount consideration.

On the following day, July 26, a circular telegram was despatched announcing that Serbia had rejected Austria's demands and had thereby shown her unwillingness to cease her subversive activities.[13] "To our regret and greatly against our wishes we are therefore compelled to force her by the sharpest methods to a complete change of her hostile attitude." Special messages were added to each Power. Germany was thanked for her sympathetic understanding. "We confidently hope that our conflict with Serbia will not lead to complications. If it does, we gratefully recognise that Germany will remember her duties as an ally and support us in an unavoidable struggle." Italy was reminded that she had recently fought the Tripoli war, and that her gains had been willingly recognised by Austria. She was also thanked for the message, which had just arrived, that she would honour her obligations as an ally. England, with her highly developed sense of justice, could not blame Austria for deciding to defend her property with the sword, and, it was hoped, would help to localise the conflict. A similar appeal was made to France, whose attitude in the Bosnian crisis was gratefully recalled.

On July 27 Berchtold telegraphed to the European capitals his comments on the Serbian reply.[14] The note, he began, was saturated with insincerity. It was clear that the Serbian Government did not seriously intend to stop the intrigues against the Monarchy. There were such far-reaching reservations and limitations, both as to the foundations of the case and in regard to particular demands, that the concessions were unimportant. In particular, on a trivial pretext, the co-operation of Austrians in the investigations of the plot of June 28

was refused. The assurances regarding Austrophobe publications amounted to a refusal. The desire that the dissolved societies should not be allowed to continue their activities under another name was ignored. Since the ultimatum contained the minimum necessitated by Serbia's attitude, her answer must be regarded as unsatisfactory. That she knew it, was proved by the order for mobilisation issued three hours before its presentation. She had behaved like a naughty child, he complained to the French Ambassador, and her dangerous pranks could be tolerated no longer.[15] On the same day the Foreign Minister obtained his master's assent to a declaration of war.[16] The Serbian reply, he wrote, was very cleverly drafted — in substance perfectly worthless, but conciliatory in form. The Entente Powers might well attempt to secure a peaceful solution of the conflict unless the situation were clearly defined. A further reason was that news of firing on Austrian troops from steamers had arrived. This imaginary attack figured in the first draft of the declaration of war approved by the Emperor, but on receipt of fuller information was omitted from the document presented at Belgrad on July 28.

. . . . . .

On July 26 Sazonoff discussed the ultimatum with the Austrian Ambassador in friendly tones. Some of the demands, he argued, were unrealisable. He suggested that they should try to work out a formula which Serbia could accept and which would satisfy Austria in principle. Next day he reported to Paris and London his affirmative answer to England's inquiry whether he approved an English invitation to a Four Power Conference in London. On the same day the Tsar replied to the appeal of the Serbian Crown Prince. "So long as the slightest hope remains of avoiding bloodshed, all our efforts will be directed to this end. If, contrary to our sincerest wishes, we fail, Your Highness

---

[13] A. VIII, 735–7.
[14] A. VIII, 774.

[15] D.D.F. XI, 438–9.
[16] A. VIII, 811–12.

can be assured that Russia will in no case be indifferent to the fate of Serbia." When Pashitch read the words he crossed himself and exclaimed: [O] God! Great, gracious, Russian Tsar!

. . . . . .

Bethmann's chief endeavour was to dissuade Russia from joining in the fray, and on the same day, July 26, he sent a warning to the Triple Entente. Austria had officially informed Russia that she aimed at no territorial gain in Serbia, but merely desired to ensure tranquillity. Yet rumours of the calling up of several classes of Russian reservists pointed to general mobilisation. "If confirmed, we shall be reluctantly compelled to take counter-measures. Our endeavour is still to localise the conflict and to preserve the peace of Europe. We therefore beg Sir Edward Grey to work in this sense at St. Petersburg." Paris was informed of his opinion that the decision for war or peace rested at the moment in Russia's hands. "We feel confident that France, sharing our wish for peace, will use her influence in St. Petersburg to this end." To Russia he wired that, in view of Austria's repudiation of territorial aims in Serbia, the preservation of peace depended on her alone. "We trust to Russia's love of peace and our traditional good relations that she will take no step which would seriously endanger European peace." Later in the day he despatched a further telegram to St. Petersburg couched in graver terms. Military measures pointed against Germany would compel her to mobilise. Mobilisation meant war against France as well as Russia. He could not believe that the latter would unleash such a conflict.

So far the Chancellor had encouraged Austria and warned Russia not to intervene. But what would England do? After the Serajevo murder, writes Otto Hammann, a high official of the Wilhelmstrasse, "he realised that, if it came to war, England would fight against us. He said so to his intimates at the beginning of July."[17]

[17] *Bilder aus der letzten Kaiserzeit* [Berlin, 1922], 75.

Lichnowsky's insistent warnings could no longer be ignored. A conference of the four Powers in London seemed the only way to avert war, wired the Ambassador on July 25. If the Serbian frontier were crossed, all was lost; for Russia would be forced to attack Austria or forever forfeit her standing with the Balkan states. The dream of localisation should be abandoned, and German policy should realise the necessity of sparing the German people a struggle in which nothing could be gained and everything might be lost. Nothing was known in Berlin of Grey's plea of a conference of four, replied Bethmann, and Germany could not drag Austria before a European tribunal. Her mediation must be confined to Austria and Russia. The necessity and possibility of localisation should be strongly pressed in St. Petersburg.

Serbia's reply, which seemed to the Kaiser to remove all need for war, encouraged the Chancellor to hope that the worst might be averted. On July 27 he reported that it accepted nearly all the points of the ultimatum; the diplomatic situation, however, was still obscure. England, France and Italy desired peace; Russia seemed ready to discuss with Austria the reserves in the document. Vienna's attitude on the latter point was unknown. "I have told all the Cabinets that we regard the Austro-Serb conflict as concerning those states alone, and have left Russia in no doubt as to the result of any military measure directed against us." Later on the same day Lichnowsky wired an urgent request from Grey. Germany should urge Austria to regard the Serbian reply as satisfactory or at any rate as a basis for discussion. In his view peace could and should be saved by Berlin. The Chancellor was so impressed by this appeal that he forwarded the telegram to Vienna. "Having already declined the English plan of a Conference, it is impossible for us entirely to reject this suggestion as well. By refusing every mediatory action we should make ourselves responsible before the whole world for the conflagration, and should appear as the real authors of war.

That would make our position impossible at home, where we must appear to have war forced upon us. Our situation is all the more difficult since Serbia has apparently given way a great deal. We cannot therefore decline the *rôle* of mediator, and must forward the English proposal to the Vienna Cabinet for consideration, while London and Paris work intensively on St. Petersburg. Ask for Count Berchtold's view of the English suggestion and of Sazonoff's wish to negotiate directly with Vienna."

Bethmann was at last thoroughly alarmed. "We have at once started mediatory action at Vienna as Sir Edward Grey desired," he telegraphed to London. "In addition to this English suggestion we have conveyed to Count Berchtold the wish of Sazonoff for a direct exchange of views." He forwarded Lichnowsky's telegram to his master and reported his action in Vienna. "It will be for Austria to decide. If we rejected every kind of mediation, while London and Paris are working on St. Petersburg, we should appear to England and the whole world responsible for the conflagration. That would render it impossible to maintain the present good feeling at home and would turn England from her neutrality." He was soon to learn that, after promising unconditional support, Germany's influence at Vienna had virtually ceased to count.

On July 28 Bethmann replied to Grey's appeal. The latter begged Germany to urge her ally to regard the Serbian reply either as satisfactory or as a basis for discussion. The first was impossible, and Austria had rejected it without consulting Berlin. "We have gone far to meet England in mediating as we have, and I count on her recognition of the fact. Whether Serbia's reply goes to the extreme limit of the possible I cannot at present say, as it has only just reached my hands. It is suspicious that she mobilised before communicating it — that suggests a bad conscience. I cannot accept Sir Edward's assumption that Austria is aiming at the overthrow of Serbia, for she has explicitly informed Russia that she seeks no territory, a declaration which has impressed Russia. Austria, as is her right and her duty, desires security that her existence shall not continue to be undermined by the Greater Serbia agitation which reached its climax in the Serajevo outrage. That has nothing to do with prestige policy or with the playing off of the Triple Alliance against the Triple Entente. While, in entire agreement with England and we hope in continuous co-operation with her in every direction, we are striving to maintain the peace of Europe, we cannot recognise the right of Russia or the Triple Entente to support Serb intrigues against Austria." In this rather stiff communication there was no hint of his growing alarm at Austrian intransigence.

A circular despatch of the same date to the Prussian representatives at the German Courts and abroad stated the Austro-German case as a guide to their attitude. The Serbian reply showed that the old policy of hostility would be continued. If Austria was not finally to surrender her position as a Great Power, she had no choice but to enforce her demands. The Russian press was preaching intervention on behalf of Serbia. But the latter, not Austria, had begun the conflict by encouraging Pan-Serb aspirations. If Russia intervened she would be solely responsible for transforming an Austro-Serb dispute, which all the other Great Powers desired to localise, into a European war. The Panslav policy aimed first at the dissolution of the Hapsburg Monarchy, next at the destruction or weakening of the Triple Alliance, and therefore the complete isolation of the German Empire. "Our own interests summon us to the side of Austria. The duty to rescue Europe if possible from a general war also moves us to support attempts at localisation, in accordance with the principles of German policy for forty-four years. If this, contrary to our hopes, is frustrated by Russian intervention, we shall have to support our neighbour with all our strength as loyal allies. We should draw the sword reluctantly, but in the calm conviction that we had no share in plunging Europe into war." Here was Germany's case, and it never changed. That she must stand by her ally on a vital issue seemed clear. That it was psychologically impossible for resurgent Russia to watch unmoved the chastisement of her *protégé* was hidden from the eyes of Berlin.

So convinced was the Chancellor that his course was right that he invited Goschen for a talk on the evening of July 28.[18] He wished Grey to know his keen desire to work with England for peace, as they had done in the last European crisis. He was urging Vienna and St. Petersburg to direct and friendly discussion. Yet if it was true that Russia had mobilised fourteen army corps in the south, he could no longer preach moderation at Vienna. Austria, who as yet was only partially mobilising, would have to take similar measures, for which Russia would be entirely responsible. When the Ambassador interjected that Austria would incur some responsibility by ignoring the Serbian reply, Bethmann rejoined that he could not discuss the document. Austria's standpoint, with which he agreed, was that her quarrel with Serbia was a purely Austrian concern, with which Russia had nothing to do. The decision of peace and war rested, not with the Kaiser, as certain French papers declared, but with Russia alone. He ended by reiterating his desire to co-operate with England and his intention to do his utmost to maintain peace. "A war between the Great Powers must be avoided," were his last words. The sincerity of his desire to avert a conflict was as obvious as his determination to keep the ring for his ally.

While stoutly championing Austrian policy in his public declarations, the Chancellor privately preached moderation at Vienna. Austria had announced that she had no territorial designs on Serbia; but, despite repeated inquiries, she had not explained her aims to her ally. Serbia's answer

had gone so far to meet her demands that a wholly intransigent attitude would gradually turn opinion against her throughout Europe. The German Ambassador was to avoid the impression that his Government wished to hold her back. It was a question of combining the suppression of Pan-Serb propaganda with the avoidance of a world war. Fuller explanations to St. Petersburg that the occupation of portions of Serbian territory would be purely temporary might induce Russia to accept the situation. If war came, the responsibility must be recognised to lie at her door. Bethmann was no better satisfied with Berchtold's attitude to Rome. Should not Austria be clearly informed, he asked Jagow, that her handling of the question of compensation was most unsatisfactory? If on the eve of a possible European conflagration she threatened to disrupt the Triple Alliance in this manner, the whole structure would become insecure. Her declaration that, in the event of permanent occupation of Serbian territory, she would consult Italy contradicted her assurance to Russia of territorial disinterestedness and would inevitably be known in St. Petersburg. Germany could not support a double policy. "I regard this as necessary," he concluded. "Otherwise we cannot continue to mediate in St. Petersburg, and ultimately we are taken in tow by Vienna. That I will not have, even at the risk of being charged with flabbiness." A sharply worded telegram in this sense was despatched the same day.

· · · · · ·

Berchtold vainly strove to localise the coming war by reiterating that Austria was acting in self-defence. When the British Ambassador suggested that the Serbian response opened the door to agreement, he rejoined quietly but firmly that Grey did not quite understand the immense significance of Austria's problems.[19] It was too late to prevent hostilities, for Austrian frontier troops had been fired on and war was being declared that very day. Compromise

18 *G. and T.* XI, 164, Goschen's report. [Gooch and Temperley, eds., *British Documents on the Origins of the War, 1898–1914.*]

19 *A.* VIII, 839–40 and *G. and T.* XI, 152–3.

on the basis of the note was inadmissible. These methods were only too familiar. They were not dealing with a civilised nation, and Austrian magnanimity had often been abused. Grey wished for peace, but the peace of Europe would not be preserved if Great Powers tried to save Serbia from chastisement. A compromise would encourage her to continue her course, which would very soon again endanger peace. The matter must be settled directly between the two parties immediately concerned. To Italy Berchtold was prepared to offer compensation under Article 7 of the Triple Alliance (though not at Austria's expense) in the unexpected event of territory being annexed.[20] This concession to the Italian standpoint, he explained to his Ambassador at Rome, was made because they were engaged in a great game, which, difficult enough in any case, would be doomed to failure without the close association of the Powers of the Triple Alliance.

· · · · · ·

Austria's declaration of war on July 28 opened the third and final act. There was now little hope. On the morning of July 29 Pourtalès telephoned that he desired to speak to the [Russian] Foreign Minister and to make an agreeable communication, though he added, *Toutefois, pas trop d'optimisme.* Germany, declared the Ambassador, approved his efforts to secure concessions from Vienna. This, however, must be kept secret, lest a divergence of views should be inferred. He implored Russia not to thwart German pressure at Vienna by premature mobilisation. When the Ambassador had gone his declaration was discussed by Sazonoff with his advisers, and the conclusion was reached that, even if honestly meant, German advice would have little effect. A second interview in the afternoon brought a less friendly communication. If Russia continued her military preparations, even without mobilising, Germany would have to mobilise and an attack would im-

[20] A. VIII, 846–8.

mediately follow. "Now I see why Austria is so intransigent," exclaimed Sazonoff. Pourtalès jumped up and cried: "I protest with all my strength against this wounding assertion." Germany, rejoined the Foreign Minister, could prove by her actions that he was wrong. At this point the grave news of the bombardment of Belgrad arrived, and the Austrian Ambassador, who was with him, was assailed with angry reproaches. Shortly after the departure of Pourtalès the Tsar telephoned to report a friendly telegram from the Kaiser. Sazonoff replied that the Ambassador's declaration a few minutes before was in another key, and the Tsar undertook to ask Berlin to clear the matter up. He authorised Sazonoff to discuss mobilisation with the War Minister and the Chief of Staff, who agreed that the chances of avoiding war with Germany were so small that general mobilisation should begin. The Tsar's approval was secured by telephone, though late in the evening he withdrew it.

Reporting to Paris the declaration that Germany would mobilise unless Russia stopped her military preparations, Sazonoff added that, as this was impossible, Russia must accelerate her arming and reckon with the apparent inevitability of war. He was most grateful to France for her assurance of support. It was highly desirable that England, without loss of time, should join France and Russia, since only in this way could a dangerous disturbance of the Balance of Power be prevented. There was now only the faintest hope of peace. "In the event of an armed conflict between Austria and Serbia," he telegraphed to Bucharest, "our intervention to avert the annihilation of Serbia will follow. That will be the purpose of our war with Austria if a conflict proves unavoidable." Rumania was promised rewards if she threw in her lot with Russia.

· · · · · ·

The [German] Chancellor was fighting a losing battle, and he knew it. On July 29 he warned both Russia and France that continuation of their military preparations would compel Germany to take action. To Sazonoff he appealed to stay his hand if Austria, in accordance with Germany's suggestion, formally reiterated that she had no territorial aims in Serbia and that the military occupation would be temporary. He pressed Vienna to regard Serbia's latest attitude as a basis for negotiations, with the occupation of a portion of her territory as a pledge. Later on the same day came the news that Russia had mobilised in the south in reply to Austria's mobilisation of eight army corps. Russian mobilisation, he commented, did not mean war as in the west, for it was a slow process; relations with Vienna were not broken off, and Russia desired if possible to avoid war. She complained that conversations were at a standstill. "We must therefore, to avert a general catastrophe or at any rate to put Russia in the wrong, earnestly desire Vienna to begin and continue the conversations."

Later in the evening of the same day, July 29, Bethmann explained his attitude to the British Ambassador on the lines of a memorandum drawn up in advance. Germany continued to strive for peace. If a Russian attack on Austria compelled her to fulfil her treaty obligations, he hoped that England would stand aside. The latter, he recognised, could not permit the destruction of France, but such was not Germany's aim. If England remained neutral, no French territory in Europe would be annexed in the event of victory. Holland's neutrality and integrity would be respected. As regards Belgium, they did not know what the action of France might compel them to do. If she did not join Germany's foes, her integrity after the war would not be touched. Such assurances seemed to render possible a further understanding with England. Her neutrality in the present conflict would facilitate a general neutrality agreement in the future. Goschen's report of this historic conversation, in which for the first time an abyss seemed to yawn under their feet, is less restrained in tone and adds a few details. To the Ambassador's

inquiry whether the promise to respect the integrity of France covered her colonial possessions Bethmann replied in the negative. It was this significant reservation which stirred Grey to the first angry words he had uttered since the crisis began.

On July 30 Bethmann forwarded to Vienna Lichnowsky's report of Grey's impressive warning of July 29, with a pathetically urgent appeal. "If Austria rejects all mediation, we are faced with a conflagration in which England is against us, Italy and Rumania in all probability not with us, and we should be two Great Powers to four." Owing to England's hostility Germany would bear the brunt. Austria's political prestige, the honour of her army, and her legitimate claims on Serbia could be adequately secured by the occupation of Belgrad or other places. It would strengthen her position in the Balkans by the humiliation of Serbia and in relation to Russia. "Under these circumstances we must urge the Vienna Cabinet to accept mediation for honourable conditions. Otherwise the responsibility for the results would be exceedingly heavy for Austria and ourselves." A second telegram forwarded a despatch conveying Sazonoff's complaint that Austria declined discussion. "We cannot ask Austria to negotiate with Serbia, with whom she is at war. But the refusal of any discussion with St. Petersburg would be a grave error, for it would actually provoke Russia to intervene, which it is Austria's chief interest to avoid. We are indeed ready to fulfil our duty as allies, but we must decline to be dragged into a world conflagration by Vienna, wantonly and in neglect of our advice. Vienna also seems to ignore our counsels in regard to Italy." In the evening a further telegram, drafted in the Chancellor's hand, renewed the appeal. If Austria was intransigent, it would hardly be possible to attribute to Russia the guilt of a European conflagration. The effect of the Chancellor's exhortations was diminished, if not absolutely nullified, by a telegram from Moltke to Conrad urging instant mobilisation against Russia, and adding that

Germany would follow suit. There is no evidence that Bethmann was aware of this communication. But that military pressure was beginning to tell on him is indicated by a wire despatched shortly before midnight countermanding for the present Tschirschky's instructions to urge the plan of a halt in Belgrad.

. . . . . .

July 30 was the day of decision for Russia and the world. At 1 A.M. Sazonoff was roused from sleep to receive the German Ambassador, who asked whether Russia would not content herself with Austria's promise not to infringe the integrity of Serbia. This was insufficient, he replied. When Pourtalès asked on what conditions Russia would cease her military preparations, he dictated a formula. "If Austria, recognising that the Austro-Serb question has become a European question, declares herself ready to eliminate from her ultimatum the points which infringe the sovereign rights of Serbia, Russia pledges herself to cease her military preparations." It was a polite refusal, and indeed the time for formulas had passed. After the Minister of War and the Chief of Staff had vainly urged the Tsar by telephone to reverse his decision of the previous day and to allow general mobilisation, Sazonoff begged for an audience and was summoned to Peterhof in the afternoon. The Chief of Staff asked for a telephone message in the event of success, so that the partial mobilisation already in progress could be instantly enlarged. "After that I will break my telephone and leave no address, in case the order is again revoked."

For an hour the Foreign Minister wrestled with his distracted master.[21] There was no more hope of peace, he began. To delay general mobilisation would be perilous. Capitulation to the Central Powers would never be forgiven and would cover the good name of the Russian people with infamy. In such a situation there was noth-

ing left but general mobilisation. The Tsar sat silent. Then, in a voice of deep emotion: "That means sending hundreds of thousands of Russians to their death. How can one fail to shrink from such a decision?" The responsibility for their precious lives, replied Sazonoff, would not rest on him. Neither he nor his Government had willed the war. They had done everything to avert it, even making sacrifices painful to Russian pride. His conscience was clear. The war was forced on Russia and Europe by the evil will of enemies who had resolved to safeguard their power by the suppression of her natural allies in the Balkans, and by the destruction of her traditional influence in that quarter, which meant condemning her to a miserable existence dependent on the caprice of the Central Powers. When he finished speaking the Tsar sat pale and silent. After a time he said, speaking with difficulty: "You are right. We have no choice but to await the attack. Inform the Chief of the Staff of my order for mobilisation." Sazonoff hurried to the telephone, and orders were despatched to every part of the empire the same afternoon a few minutes after six.[22] In the words of Dobrorolski, head of the Mobilisation Department, the prologue of the great historic drama had begun. This decisive step was taken without consulting France, whose counsels of caution were ignored.[23]

July 31 brought a momentary ray of hope when Austria at last announced her willingness to discuss the ultimatum to Serbia. In expressing his satisfaction, Sazonoff suggested that the negotiations should take place in London and that the Great Powers should co-operate. "We hope the English Government will take the lead in these discussions and thereby earn the gratitude of Europe," he telegraphed to his Ambassadors. "It would be a great help if Austria stopped her military operations on Serbian territory." It was too late, for on that morning St. Petersburg was plastered

---

[21] [Sazonov] *Fateful Years* [London, 1928], ch. 9; *Imperialismus*, V, 196–8.

[22] Dobrorolski, *Die Mobilmachung der Russischen Armee, 1914* [Berlin, 1922], p. 29.

[23] D.D.F. XI, 261–2.

with mobilisation orders. When Pourtalès asked for explanations he was informed that the decision was purely precautionary. Russia would take no irrevocable step, and peace could be preserved if Germany were willing to urge moderation at Vienna. The same afternoon Germany proclaimed *Drohende Kriegsgefahr* [threatening danger of war] and summoned Russia to demobilise. Unless a satisfactory answer was made within twelve hours, she would mobilise herself.

. . . . . .

On July 30, after reporting Grey's desire for the mediation of the four less interested Powers and his broad hint of British intervention, Germany attempted to put on the brake. On the same day the Austrian Ambassador in Berlin reported growing nervousness due to the attitude of Italy, and the desire for a generous settlement of the question of compensation. Unless the Triple Alliance held together, the chances of victory in a great struggle were diminished. These moderating counsels were counteracted by a telegram from the Austrian Military Attaché to Conrad reporting Moltke's urgent desire for immediate general mobilisation. If tremors were felt in the Wilhelmstrasse, there was no sign of weakness in the Ballplatz, even when Russia mobilised on all fronts. Berchtold had made up his mind after June 28, had counted the cost, and never looked back. "Conscious of my grave duties to my realm," telegraphed Francis Joseph to the Kaiser on July 31, "I have ordered the mobilisation of my entire forces. The operations of my army against Serbia cannot be interrupted by the threatening challenge of Russia. A fresh rescue of Serbia by Russian intervention would involve the most serious consequences for my territories, and therefore I cannot possibly allow it. I am aware of the significance of the decisions which I have reached, trusting in divine justice and in the assurance that your forces will stand in unflinching loyalty for my realm and the Triple Alliance."

On the same day, July 31, a final Ministerial Council was held.[24] When the German Ambassador had communicated the English suggestion on July 30, began the Foreign Minister, he had at once declared that hostilities against Serbia must proceed. The official reply had not been drafted, but it would contain three points. Military operations would continue; the English proposal could not be discussed unless the Russian mobilisation were countermanded; the Austrian demands would have to be accepted *en bloc* and must not be discussed. In such cases the Powers always tried to water down demands. France, England and Italy would take the Russian view, and Lichnowsky was no friend of Austria. A victory of prestige would not be worth while. The mere occupation of Belgrad, even if Russia consented, would be useless. Russia would emerge as the saviour of Serbia, who in two or three years would attack under much more unfavourable circumstances. Berchtold's plan of a polite refusal was approved by his colleagues, to whom the mere thought of a renewal of the Ambassadors' Conference of 1912–13 was odious. Passing to Italy he reported her opinion that the conflict was provoked by Austria; but her attitude, he explained, was determined by her desire for compensation under Article 7 of the treaty. Such a claim would only arise if Austria occupied Turkish territory, provisionally or otherwise, since according to the spirit of the treaty only Ottoman territory was in question. Italy, on the other hand, argued that the whole Balkan peninsula was concerned, and Germany agreed with her. The Italian Government declared the coming war contrary to Italian interests, since in the event of success Austrian power in the Balkans would be increased. To the demand for compensation he had replied that territorial acquisitions were not contemplated, and that it would be time to discuss it if they were made. It was decided that, if Italy fulfilled her duty as an ally, she might have Valona, in which case

[24] A. VIII, 976–9.

Austria would secure the dominant influence in North Albania. Compensation would only be made, he explained to his master, if Italy was friendly in a localised war or fulfilled her obligations in a European struggle.

. . . . . .

Russia's general mobilisation, decreed on the afternoon of July 30 and known next morning, produced the same effect in Germany as the German violation of Belgian neutrality was to produce in England. Since war was already regarded as virtually inevitable the news came as a relief, for no better cry could be desired to rally the nation than the threat of a Russian invasion. *Drohende Kriegsgefahr* was proclaimed, and Russia was summoned to countermand all war measures against Austria and Germany within twelve hours. France was asked whether she would remain neutral in a Russo-German war. If so — though such an answer was improbable — the fortresses of Toul and Verdun should be surrendered as a pledge for the duration of the war. In announcing to Rome the imminence of a conflict on two fronts, the Chancellor added that Germany counted on the fulfilment of her treaty obligations. In his mediatorial *rôle* at Vienna, he wired to Lichnowsky, he had gone to the utmost limit of what was possible with a sovereign state and an ally. Before Austria's reply was ready Russia had mobilised her whole forces. This was aimed at Germany not less than Austria, and it was impossible to stand with folded arms. The Ambassador was to explain the sequence of events. There was no choice but to proclaim *Drohende Kriegsgefahr*. To delay would be to expose Eastern Germany to invasion. The provocation of mobilising against Germany while she was mediating in Vienna at Russia's request was so strong that no German would understand it if sharp measures were not adopted. The Kaiser telegraphed to Francis Joseph that he was ready, in discharge of his obligations as an ally, to begin war against Russia and France at once. Austria should direct her chief offensive against Russia,

not against Serbia, whose *rôle* in the immense conflict was quite secondary. And everything should be done to secure the co-operation of Italy.

On August 1 the Chancellor addressed the Bundesrat. "Against our will and despite all our efforts," he began, "unless God works a miracle at the eleventh hour, a crisis of unexampled gravity threatens the peace of Europe and Germany." It was not only the right but the duty of Austria to take action against the Great Serbian movement which menaced her existence. It was a German interest that Austria should not fall in a struggle with the Southern Slavs, over whom Russia aspired to play the part of Protector. If the Austrian state were destroyed, the roots of the German Empire would be attacked. That had been its policy for thirty years. Thus, when Austria announced that she must act, they had replied: What you decide is not our business, but if the *casus foederis* arises we are of course at your side. Serbia's response had made concessions but had also declined important demands. Austria's experience had proved that mere assurances were worthless and that concrete guarantees must be secured.

The desire to localise the conflict, continued the Chancellor, was approved by all the Powers except Russia, who made secret military preparations, in the first instance against Austria. At Russia's request they had mediated in Vienna, asking Austria solemnly to reiterate that she sought no territorial conquest, that she merely desired relief from Great Serbian propaganda, and that the occupation of territory was only a pledge for the fulfilment of her demands. England's mediation, which they had supported at Vienna, took the same course. While these negotiations were in progress Russia had mobilised against Austria, and the Kaiser had warned the Tsar of the consequences. Austria's reply to the German and English request was due on the previous day. She had at any rate resumed direct discussions with Russia. At this moment the latter's mobilisation on all fronts compelled Germany to move. Russia pretended that it was not an act of hostility against her, but to accept this view would be to sin against the security of the Fatherland. With an admirable and almost culpable tranquillity Germany had watched the military measures of Russia and France which prepared the way for mobilisation. She had risked losing the advantage of her quicker mobilisation: to wait longer was to invite invasion. An ultimatum had been sent to Russia and an inquiry to France. If the replies, as he expected, were unsatisfactory, Germany would declare war. "We have not willed the war: it is forced upon us."

. . . . . .

On the afternoon of August 1 Pourtalès asked to see the [Russian] Foreign Minister, who remarked: "Probably he brings me the declaration of war." Would the Government give a favourable answer to yesterday's note? he inquired. Sazonoff turned the question aside, adding that, though the mobilisation could not be suspended, Russia was prepared to continue negotiations. Taking a folded paper from his pocket, the Ambassador repeated his question, emphasising the gravity of refusal. With increasing excitement he repeated the question a third time, and received the reply: *Je n'ai pas d'autre réponse à vous donner*. Deeply moved and with trembling hand he presented a declaration of war. Then he burst into tears, embraced the Minister, and left the room. Germany, telegraphed Sazonoff to London, was striving to place the responsibility for the breach on Russian shoulders. Russia had been forced to mobilise, since Austria was spinning out the discussions and had bombarded Belgrad. Germany had no right to doubt the Tsar's assurance that he would commit no provocation so long as the negotiations with Austria continued, and that Russia would welcome any solution compatible with the dignity and independence of Serbia. Any other attitude would have destroyed the European equilibrium by confirming German hegemony.

Sazonoff, like the Foreign Ministers in the other capitals, was convinced that he had no alternative. All of them wanted peace, but they desired other things still more. He inherited a tradition from which he had neither the power nor the wish to depart. Russia's inability to take up the challenge in 1909 was a bitter memory, and no one could expect her to submit to humiliation again. By 1914, thanks to military reorganisation and a series of good harvests, she had regained her self-confidence. Since the main purpose of the Triple Entente, as defined by Sazonoff, was to prevent the domination of Europe by Germany, now was the time to make a stand. As Berchtold saw the long arm of Russia in the Serajevo murders, so the Russian Foreign Minister envisaged the ultimatum as a blow at Nicholas II not less than at Peter Karageorgevich. Now that Bulgaria was lost Serbia was Russia's acknowledged outpost in the Balkans, and Sazonoff spoke of the Serbs as "our children." Had Russia left her *protégé* for a second time to the tender mercies of Austria, she would have forfeited her historic claim to be the champion of the Slav races and have handed over the Near East to the domination of the Central Powers. Though bound by no treaty obligation to intervene, she could no more be expected to remain neutral in face of an Austrian attack on Belgrad than England in face of a German violation of Belgian neutrality. The same instinctive pride of a Great Power which prompted Vienna to throw down the glove compelled St. Petersburg to pick it up. It is true that, while Austria fought under the banner of self-preservation, Russia, whom nobody threatened, marched out to battle in the name of prestige. But in the accepted scale of national values prestige, honour and security are motive forces of equal weight. A few experienced public servants, among them Witte, Rosen and Taube, convinced that Russia was unequal to a conflict with the Central Powers, disapproved an active policy in the Near East; but they possessed no influence at Court, in the army or among the people. Russia's responsibility for the catastrophe was greater than Sazonoff was prepared to admit, for her championship of Pan-Serb ambitions was Austria's chief anxiety. Yet the ultimate cause of the conflagration was the rivalry of two proud Empires, which was far older than the Austro-Serb feud. Thus when the hour of decision arrived, and the whole world was looking on, neither side cared or dared to draw back.

. . . . . .

That Germany declared war against Russia on August 1 while Austria waited till August 6 was due to military considerations alone. It is a legend that the stronger partner, thirsting for the fray, hustled the weaker; for the policy was made in Vienna, not in Berlin, and at the eleventh hour Bethmann endeavoured to rein in the runaway steed. Berchtold and his colleagues, in possession of the German promise of support, had gone straight ahead, resolved to perish rather than retreat. Perhaps only a timely and categorical declaration of England's intention to intervene could have held them back. It was natural that Serbia should aspire to unite under her sceptre the discontented Southern Slav subjects of her neighbour, should use their rankling grievances to foster the Pan-Serb idea, and should look to Russia for assistance as in similar circumstances Cavour had looked to France. It was equally natural that Austria, who coveted no man's territory, and who, alone of the eight Great Powers of the world, possessed no colonies, should resolve to defend herself against the openly proclaimed ambition to rob her of provinces which she had held for centuries. In taking up what he regarded as a challenge, Berchtold was speaking for his countrymen and acting as almost every other Austrian statesman would have done in his place. By common consent he had displayed unusual patience during the Balkan war, but the ultimatum of 1913 was a warning that there were limits. These limits had now been passed. "So just was the cause of Austria held to be," reported Sir Maurice de Bunsen, the British Ambassador, "that

it seemed to her people inconceivable that any country should place itself in her path, or that questions of mere policy or prestige should be regarded anywhere as superseding the necessity which had arisen to exact summary vengeance for the crime of Serajevo."[25]

That Serbia, flushed with victory over Turks and Bulgars and encouraged by promises of Russian support, would remain content with the frontiers of 1913 Berchtold did not believe. If a real reconciliation had ever been practicable since the change of dynasty at Belgrad in 1903, the time had passed when he was called to the helm, and for the rough handling of the Southern Slav subjects of Francis Joseph he was not responsible. The conciliatory Baernreither was a voice crying in the wilderness. Austria's intransigence after Serajevo, which surprised and shocked the world, is only intelligible in the light of her experiences and emotions since 1908. At the close of the Bosnian crisis Serbia had promised to be a good neighbour, but she had not kept her word and her intimacy with Russia was notorious. For Austria to sit with folded arms and wait till her enemies in combination felt strong enough to carry out their programme of dismemberment was to proclaim her impotence and invite attack. "If you pull up twice at the fence," observed the fiery Conrad, "the third time your horse will not jump." The carefully organised murder of the heir to the throne appeared to demand some striking vindication of the authority of the State.

The ultimatum was admittedly a gamble, for the localisation of the conflict was not seriously expected. If it failed, the realm of the Hapsburgs would disappear, and the Emperor remarked that they would be lucky if they got off with a black eye. It was envisaged as a strictly defensive action, offering the only chance of escape from a peril certain to increase. "The Serajevo crime was simply one of the latest examples of the work of destruction organised against

[25] G. and T. XI, 357.

us, of the sapping and mining which was to blow up the home in which we dwelt. . . .[26] The Monarchy was faced by the alternative: A free hand for the housebreaker or the demand for security. On the rejection of the latter a fight for life was all that remained." Here is Berchtold's case stated many years later in his own words. That the war was lost and the Hapsburg Empire disappeared never altered his conviction that no other course was open in 1914. Better death with honour than a lingering decline! *Si fractus inlabatur orbis, impavidum ferient ruinae.*

. . . . . .

Could England now be kept out of the fray? On August 2 Lichnowsky wired that Belgium would decide the issue. "If we violate her neutrality, and a war against the Belgians results, I do not believe that the Government in view of the outburst of opinion could remain neutral much longer. If we respect her neutrality, it is possible that England will remain neutral if we use our victory over France with moderation." The appeal was fruitless, for the Schlieffen plan barred the way. . . .

The Chancellor's historic speech to the Reichstag on August 4 was delivered before the English declaration of war reached Berlin.[27] A peace-loving nation, he began, desired to continue its work, but Russia had set a torch to the house. She alone had opposed the localisation of the Austro-Serb conflict. Germany had warmly supported England's efforts to mediate between Vienna and St. Petersburg, and had herself gone as far in mediation as was compatible with the alliance. When Russia, despite German warnings, ordered general mobilisation and France started military preparations, it would have been a crime to wait for the attack. "Gentlemen, we are now in a state of necessity, and necessity knows no law. Our troops have occupied Luxemburg, and perhaps crossed the Belgian frontier.

That is contrary to international law. The French Government declared that it would respect the neutrality of Belgium so long as its opponents did the same. But we know that France was ready to advance. France could wait: we could not. A French attack on our flank on the lower Rhine might have been disastrous. Thus we were compelled to ignore the legitimate protests of the Luxemburg and Belgian Governments. The wrong we thereby commit we will try to make good as soon as our military goal is attained. Whoever is threatened as we are and is fighting for his life can only consider one thing — how to hack his way through." The day ended with the fateful telegram from London and the agitated conversation with Goschen, in which the Chancellor bitterly complained that Great Britain, just for a scrap of paper, was going to make war on a kindred nation who desired nothing better than to be friends with her.

Bethmann, like the other statesmen of 1914, never publicly acknowledged by tongue or pen any error of policy, but he was too conscientious to be entirely satisfied with himself. "When one comes to the question of responsibility for this war," he remarked to Theodor Wolff early in 1915, "we must candidly admit that we have our share of it.[28] To say that I am oppressed by this thought would be to say too little. It never leaves me, I live in it. I am not speaking of this or the other diplomatic move which might perhaps have been made differently." Perhaps Bülow, he added, with his immense resourcefulness might have found his way out of the crisis.

The Hamlet of modern Germany, "The philosopher of Hohenfinow," as he was called, had inherited a situation which he was powerless to change. Like Grey he was a great gentleman and a sincere lover of peace; but he was an amateur in diplomacy and he was never master in his own house. He longed for the friendship of England, but he was forbidden to pay the price.

[26] [Steinitz,] *Rings um Sazonow*, 51.
[27] Bethmann Hollweg, *Kriegsreden* [Stuttgart and Berlin, 1919], 3–12.
[28] Theodor Wolff, *The Eve of 1914* [London, 1935], 619–22.

With France there was nothing to be done. Italy was a member of the Triple Alliance only in name. The Potsdam agreement was a false dawn, for the incurable Austro-Russian rivalry remained. Thus, confronted by the Triple Entente, Germany was forced to lean ever more heavily on her only dependable ally, who naturally turned the altered relationship to account. Austria became the rider and Germany the horse. The paradox that the stronger Power should be taken in tow by the weaker was the result of the blunders which left Germany without other influential friends. When the testing time came in 1914 the policy of Berlin, as of Paris and London, was governed by the nightmare of isolation. Austria had determined to remove the Serbian menace. If she ceased to be a Great Power through the loss of her southern provinces Germany would stand alone, wedged in between a hostile Russia growing rapidly stronger and an irreconcilable France. From such a prospect even the mightiest of European states shrunk back in alarm. In the Bulgarian crisis of the 'eighties Bismarck had bluntly told his ally that he would not fight for her Balkan ambitions; but at that time the wire to St. Petersburg was working and he possessed the friendship of England, which his clumsy successors had lost. On the other hand he had declared in his apologia, in a passage which every German statesman knew by heart, that the maintenance of Austria as a Great Power was for Germany a condition of the European equilibrium for which the peace of the country might be sacrificed with an easy conscience in case of need.

When Francis Joseph inquired whether he might rely on the support of Germany, William II and his Chancellor answered that he could. A refusal would have devitalised if not actually destroyed the partnership of 1879. Moreover the Kaiser's appearance in shining armour at the side of the aged Emperor in 1909 had compelled Russia to keep the peace, and it was hoped that a fresh demonstration of solidarity might perhaps produce an equally satis-factory result. The mistake of Berlin was not in promising aid but in allowing Berchtold alone to steer the ship. In entering on such a perilous course, where the existence of the German nation was at stake, the Wilhelmstrasse should have insisted on consultation throughout. The decision whether there was to be a world war, declares Bethmann, lay with Russia, and the blame was hers. He failed to realise that she had no real choice. The situation had changed since the easy triumphs of the Bosnian crisis. If she lacked Austria's excuse of self-preservation, she was driven forward by peremptory considerations of prestige. She had recovered her strength and self-confidence. Serbia was flushed by her recent victories. England had drawn ever closer to her friends. The localisation of an Austro-Serb conflict was too much to expect. Bethmann himself confesses his mistake in believing that Russia would shrink from the *ultima ratio,* and that England would prefer her friendship to the peace of the world. Warnings had reached him, but they were unheeded. Every war is a gamble, and the conflagration implicit in the German response to Austria's appeal was among the most desperate ventures in history. It is true that a struggle between the Teuton and the Slav was considered in Berlin to be almost inevitable; and, if it had to come, the German General Staff preferred 1914 to a later date, when Russia's strategic railways on the Polish front would be complete and the Three Years Service in France in full operation. Thus the civil and military authorities were ready for all eventualities if Russia intervened. Yet when all allowances are made for the difficulties of the situation and the inexperience of the Chancellor in the maze of foreign affairs, there is little excuse for stumbling into an undesired conflict when the best cards were in the hands of the foe. Whether Bülow or Tirpitz, his bitterest critics, would have done better is another question. It was a misfortune for the world that post-Bismarckian Germany produced no statesman of the first rank.

Economic and Social Causes
of the War

K. ZILLIACUS

Born in Kobe, Japan, of a Swedish-Finnish father and a Scotch-American
mother, Konne Zilliacus went to school in Brooklyn, Finland, Sweden, and
England, but returned to the United States to be graduated from Yale at the
head of his class in 1915. After fighting in the First World War, he was a
member of the Information Section of the League of Nations secretariat between
the wars. During the Second World War he worked in the British Ministry of
Information, and since 1945 has been a member of the House of Commons.
Because of his vigorous criticism of the Labor Government's foreign policy he
was expelled from the Labor party in 1949, but was later readmitted, although
his extreme left-wing views have identified him with communism. His book,
from which the following extract is taken, is subtitled, *A History of Secret
Diplomacy* and its message is that those who tackled reconstruction after 1919
failed because they tried to restore the pre-war economic, social, and international conditions which had caused war in 1914.

WHY BRITAIN WENT TO WAR

IT IS NOT necessary at this date to labour
the point that this propaganda [that
Britain went to war because Germany violated Belgian neutrality] was false in every
particular, and that the governing class in
Great Britain and every other belligerent
country cared nothing at all for international law, or treaty obligations, or the
rights of small nations. The *Times* was
right when it wrote, on December 4, 1914,
"We have always fought for the Balance of
Power. We are fighting for it today."[1]
Sir Arnold Wilson put the same point
when he said in the House of Commons

on February 24, 1936, in the course of a
glowing tribute to Sir Edward (then Lord)
Grey, that he would "go down in history
as a man who was the foremost in keeping
the bond of this country when he thought
that the interests of the country required it."

This does not imply any lack of personal
sincerity on the part of the Liberal government and the Foreign Office. They were
intensely sincere in identifying their view
of "national interests" with "honour" and
"right." Nor was it more wrong for the
Asquith-Grey government to play power
politics in defence of imperialism than for
any other great power to do the same.

[1] *The Times* insisted on this point repeatedly —
see, *e.g.*, its leader of March 8, 1915. See also the
Spectator of December 19, 1914. The Conservative
party, in Mr. Bonar Law's letter to Mr. Asquith
of August 2, 1914, promising full support in case
of war, said not one word of Belgium, but urged
that "it would be fatal to the honour and security
of the United Kingdom to hesitate in supporting
France and Russia at the present juncture." Professor Gilbert Murray, in his semi-official Foreign
Office propaganda pamphlet referred to above, argued that in no circumstances could Great Britain
allow Germany to weaken France.

But it does mean that there was a vast gulf between what the rulers of Great Britain were really fighting for and what they persuaded themselves and the British people that they were fighting for. The same discrepancy existed in all the belligerent countries. Its nature is indicated in the conclusion of this chapter and made clearer in the next chapter.

At this stage in our analysis of events it is sufficient to point out that whereas all the belligerents believed they were fighting in self-defence in a war that had been thrust upon them, each of them was in fact fighting a "preventive" war.

Austria-Hungary declared war on Serbia to prevent Pan-Serbian agitation from disrupting the Empire.

Russia mobilized against Austria to prevent Serbia from being crushed, for this would have meant Austro-German hegemony in the Balkans and Turkey and the end of Russian imperialist expansion in Southeast Europe and Asia Minor.

Germany backed Austria to prevent her from being crushed and Russian hegemony established in the Balkans, as that would have meant the end of German imperialist expansion in South-east Europe and Asia Minor.

France supported Russia on the principle of "after Sadowa, Sedan" — i.e., if Germany won her war against Russia, she would become master of Central Europe from the Baltic to the Balkans, and would then be strong enough to help herself to French colonies.

Britain declared war on Germany because if Germany won her war against France and Russia she would become master of all Europe, and strong enough to help herself to British colonies.

Each side was defending its imperialist interests by preventing the balance of power from being tipped in favour of its opponents. These imperialist interests were in the last analysis the private interests of finance and monopoly capital, which, through the influence of the plutocracy on governments and public opinion, were identified in the minds of the rulers with "national honour and vital interests." There were, of course, other factors in the situation, and the psychological process by which promoting vested interests in imperialism and war preparations is transmuted in men's minds into loyalty to religious, philanthropic, and patriotic ideals is complex and largely unconscious.

But the more closely world affairs before World War I are studied, the clearer it becomes that the pursuit of profits by finance capital was the chief "social dynamic" behind the drive for imperialism, protectionism,[2] and armaments. It was these vested interests that put up most of the money for Navy and Air and Empire leagues, Colonial Societies, and similar patriotic poisoners of public opinion. It was the plutocracy that owned part of the press and influenced most of the press through the control of advertising. It was the plutocracy that financed the British capitalist parties, whose leaders and members of Parliament were almost exclusively drawn from the class that lives by rent, interest, and profit.

These people did not believe in the rightness of what they were doing as much as they were unconscious of the possibility of doing differently. Their framework of experience was to them coincident with the limits of reality. Anything beyond was idle dreams or pernicious rubbish. They accepted the economic foundations of society as part of the order of nature, and the private profit-seeking motive as almost divinely inspired. Therefore the social dynamic of the drift to war operated below the threshold of their consciousness, in a sphere that they regarded as not subject to political control. It followed that their attitude to war was fatalistic. The idea that war was a man-made thing and that its causes could be ascertained and eliminated

---

[2] Tariff wars played a big part in the growing tension between Germany and Russia and between Austria and Serbia. They were started and maintained for the usual mixed motives — power politics and vested interests.

belonged, in their view, to the category of "idle dreams" and "pernicious rubbish." For to tackle the problem seriously meant disturbing the vested interests by which they lived and which to them seemed part of the order of nature.

Nothing is more striking in the story of how civilization collapsed in World War I than the sense of helplessness, of the governments and diplomats being mere puppets in the grip of blind forces. Mr. G. M. Trevelyan, in his *Lord Grey of Fallodon,* quotes the remark by Grey that "I used to hope that I was meant to keep the country out of war. But perhaps my real business was to bring her into it unitedly." It is not difficult to detect in this mystic resignation a refuge from the haunting sense of futility and failure.

As for the peoples, they were nothing at all, even in the most advanced democracies, except cannon fodder. No government ever dreamed of consulting them on matters of foreign policy, or hesitated to deceive them if they were presumptuous enough to question the ways of their rulers. All governments took it for granted that they would let themselves be butchered in unlimited quantities when the game of power politics made war necessary.

CONCLUSION

If even today public opinion learnt the lesson of our failure to preserve peace in 1914, it might understand why we failed again in 1939. In that case we should have a better chance to win the peace after World War II than we did after World War I. For that lesson goes to the roots of the present situation, and if we profit by it we still have time to apply our hardly won wisdom to the new peace settlement.

It will take all the chapters of this book to reveal the full lesson. But let us endeavour to indicate the conclusions that would appear to emerge from what has been said hitherto. In doing so it will make things clearer to go from the particular to the general, beginning with specific criticisms of British foreign policy before 1914.

Let us take first the criticism that it was wrong for Great Britain to conclude the military and naval agreements. This is an argument for isolation. "Splendid isolation" was abandoned, as shown in the early part of this chapter, because Great Britain had ceased to be strong enough to defend the whole British Empire against all comers. And the British ruling class believed, and had persuaded public opinion to believe, that colonies were worth acquiring and keeping.

A variant of this view is that France and Great Britain should have remained neutral, and let Germany and Austria-Hungary defeat Russia. But in that case Germany would have become the master of all Central and Eastern Europe from the Baltic to the Balkans, and would have compelled France and Great Britain to surrender their colonial empires.

A Russian defeat, or a British refusal to lend the Czar the money to put down the first (1905) Russian Revolution, might, it is true, have resulted in a successful revolution in Russia that would have led to the democratization of Germany. But that would have meant a double risk. In the first place, it would have weakened the Entente temporarily in comparison with the central powers, and the latter might have exploited the situation to acquire a colony or two, or to push on in the Balkans. In the second place, once a revolution begins, one never knows how far it will go.

The governing class in pre-1914 days had not begun to be seriously disturbed about the stability of the social order. But at the back of their minds there was a little uneasiness that was now and again expressed in words. One catches glimpses from time to time of a social motive in foreign affairs. The previous chapter quoted Cecil Rhodes's view of imperialism as an antidote to social unrest. Lord Salisbury in the '90's complained:

Unfortunately we no longer live in the time of Pitt. Then the aristocracy was in power, and we could pursue an active policy which made England, after the Congress of

Vienna, the richest and most respected of European Powers. Now the democracy rules, and has introduced a *régime* of persons and parties which has made every English Government dependent, unconditionally, on the *aura popularis*. . . . This generation can only be taught by events.

The first treaty of the Triple Alliance, concluded in 1882, began with a preamble stating that the contracting parties had made this agreement in order "to increase the guarantees of general peace, to fortify the monarchical principle, and thereby to assure the unimpaired maintenance of the social and political order in their respective States."

The Kaiser, in commenting on the idea of disarmament in connection with the First Hague Conference (1899), objected that it would mean "handing over his towns to anarchy and democracy."

Isvolski, at the Second Hague Conference (1907), dismissed disarmament as "a dream of Jews, Socialists, and hysterical women."

At an early stage (July 23) of the negotiations during the fateful twelve days that swept the world into Armageddon, Sir Edward Grey warned the Austrian Ambassador that "if four great States, Austria-Hungary, Germany, Russia and France, should be involved in war," there would be economic bankruptcy and "the industrial centres in an uproar, so that in most countries, no matter who were victorious, many an existing institution would be swept away."

The Austrian Ambassador reports as follows his last talk with Sir Edward Grey, when all was lost and war was upon Britain:

Grey is in despair that his efforts to maintain the peace have gone to ruin. Again and again he said of the war, "I hate it, I hate it!" He recalled all the efforts we had made together, in the previous year, during the Balkan Conference. He had earnestly hoped that, once the present dangers were passed, it might be possible to preserve the peace for years. "I was quite ready if ever Russia had been aggressive — in the case of France it was

not likely that she should — to stand by Germany, and that we might come to some sort of understanding between the Powers. Now all that was shattered, and universal war, with all its horrible and revolting consequences, had broken out. . . . It was the greatest step towards Socialism that could possibly have been made. . . . We should have Labour Governments in every country after this."

This cry of the heart shows Sir Edward Grey's passionate sincerity about peace. But it also shows that the culminating horror of the world war to his mind was the danger of an advance towards socialism.

A Foreign Secretary who felt like that was not going to take any risk of encouraging revolution, either in Russia or anywhere else. He would prefer the certainty of power politics ultimately ending in a world war. And his feelings were not peculiar. They were typical of his Government, his diplomatic service, and his class.

A further criticism of British policy in those fatal three weeks was the failure to put pressure on Russia to postpone mobilization. But Lowes Dickinson, who is inclined to agree with this criticism, points out that Russia had the assurance of French support and

would have risked war even without any certainty of British support. For consistently from the beginning she had made it clear that she would not stand by to see Serbia crushed by Austria. It is possible that Sir Edward was afraid that to stop Russia's preparations might encourage Germany to precipitate the war.[3]

The evidence adduced earlier in this chapter makes it clear that Russia, although the general staff finally forced the Czar's hand, did her best for some time to urge conciliation on Serbia and to secure a peaceful settlement, and that it was chiefly Germany and Austria that needed restraining — although the former did try to hold back Austria when she discovered — too late — that the British Government was going to stand by France. Bethmann-Holl-

[3] Goldsworthy Lowes Dickinson, *The International Anarchy, 1904–1914*, Century, 1926, p. 458.

weg says in his *Memoirs* that if he had only known earlier where Britain stood he could have restrained Austria and his own militarists and there would have been no war. In other words, if all concerned in Germany and Austria had known beforehand that they could not get away with a war, they might have kept the peace. Of the two, the Austrian Government, smarting under the assassination of the Archduke and really frightened of Pan-Serb propaganda, bore the chief, direct responsibility for turning the last diplomatic crisis into World War I.

There were occasions, notably during the Balkan Wars, when all the powers concerned had met in conference, when Sir Edward Grey helped to keep the peace by being careful, as Lowes Dickinson writes about the final crisis, "not to give the impression either that England would keep out of the war, under all circumstances, or that she would, necessarily, come in." But in 1914 this ambiguity, combined with the confusion and delays of diplomacy, played straight into the hands of those who pushed Europe over the edge.

On the other hand, there were two reasons why the British Government would not commit itself wholly to the Franco-Russian alliance. In the first place it was reluctant to give up the illusion of a free hand for the certainty of commitment, because it feared it would not get any corresponding measure of control over the foreign policies of the countries to which it was committed. Its members were genuine Liberals, in the sense of being reluctant and half-hearted about imperialism and power politics, and acquiescing in them only as the lesser evil (the greater evil being in their view the risks attaching to democracy in foreign politics).

In the second place, public opinion was isolationist and opposed to any commitments of any kind. Why, then, it may be asked, did not the Liberal government take the people into its confidence, and begin to educate them as to the necessity for an alliance to maintain the balance of power? Why did this course appear to it a greater evil than power politics and secret diplomacy?

The answer is that no one could tell where this process of democratizing foreign policy would stop. Many Liberals, and almost all Radicals and Labour men, were already displaying hostility to armaments and colonial imperialism. A certain Norman Angell had written an inconveniently plausible and popular book, in which he pointed out that the arguments of imperialists that colonies were necessary to the livelihood of the people were a "great illusion." Socialists had completed this demonstration by showing that the arms race and colonial buccaneering were inspired by the influence, of a more or less corrupt character, of big vested interests on governments and the press. It had not been altogether easy to keep public opinion from being too much interested in what was going on in Egypt, Morocco, Persia, and Tripoli. It would be optimistic to believe that the more the common people knew of these things, the readier they would be to pay in taxes, and finally in blood, for imperialism and power politics. For imperialism and power politics are the interest of plutocracy, but not of the common people. But the British Government saw no way of abandoning these things without shaking the foundations of the existing social order — that is, without incurring risks that were literally unthinkable.

To this day the British Foreign Office, unlike the rest of the civil service, is recruited by selection in addition to examination, and is the almost exclusive preserve of the upper middle class and the aristocracy.[4] Before World War I this was wholly the case, and the Foreign Office was in complete charge of British foreign policy. Sir Edward Grey was little more than a dignified mouthpiece for his permanent officials. He had no policy of his own. He acted only as a sort of emollient and brake on their conduct of foreign policy, and as

[4] The situation is not likely to be substantially changed by the much-heralded reform and fusion of the diplomatic and consular services.

an intermediary between them and the few members of the Cabinet who were adjudged worthy to be let into the secret. . . .

In those days it was the governing class and the diplomats and military men who had a monopoly in the related domains of foreign affairs and defence. They were experts, who accepted unquestioningly the premises of imperialism and were skilful in playing the game of power politics that revolved about imperialism. They knew that public opinion was beginning to question the premises, and therefore tried to keep it ignorant of details, lest public opinion should learn too much and put an end to the whole game. . . .

The Foreign Office, by tradition, training, and class origin, saw "national interests" in terms of the interests of the plutocracy.

But let us not underestimate the difficulties of the Liberal government. It came into office in a world where international anarchy, power politics, and the arms race were the only known method of conducting international affairs, and where British imperialism was a going concern and faced by rival imperialisms. Liberals who might want to change these things knew they would have to fight the Foreign Office, the Colonial Office, and the fighting services, as well as the solidly imperialist and power-politics Conservative party.

Behind these hostile forces, and the press and propaganda they could command, were the plutocracy that subscribed most of the party funds to both the Liberal and Conservative parties. There was the difficulty that foreign powers would mistake concessions and conciliation for weakness, and merely ask for more. Although it was dangerous to educate public opinion out of its isolationism, it was difficult to innovate without the support of a militant and informed opinion. Liberals were impaled on the horns of an insoluble dilemma, and were borne along to World War I struggling vainly to free themselves.

The root of their difficulty and the fundamental fact that governed the situation were clearly stated as far back as 1903 by Mr. J. A. Hobson in his classic work, *Imperialism*:

It is not too much to say that the modern foreign policy of Great Britain is primarily a struggle for profitable markets of investment. To a larger extent every year Great Britain is becoming a nation living upon a tribute from abroad, and the classes who enjoy this tribute have an ever-increasing incentive to employ the public policy, the public purse, and the public force to extend the field of their private investments, and to safeguard and improve their existing investments. This is, perhaps, the most important fact in modern politics, and the obscurity in which it is wrapped constitutes the gravest danger to our State.

What is true of Great Britain is true likewise of France, Germany, the United States, and of all countries in which modern capitalism has placed large surplus savings in the hands of a plutocracy. . . . Thus we reach the conclusion that Imperialism is the endeavour of the great controllers of industry to broaden the channel for the flow of their surplus wealth by seeking foreign markets and foreign investments to take off the goods and capital they cannot sell or use at home.[5]

There could be no solution of that difficulty so long as economic life was based on the private profit-seeking motive, which, magnified and concentrated through finance capital, exercised a decisive political influence without accepting any public control.

One school of German socialists did indeed invent the comforting doctrine of "ultra-imperialism." They believed that finance capital would tend to coalesce more and more across frontiers, into international trusts and combines that would lay the economic foundations for some form of world government based on the international exploitation of colonial territories. There were certain developments in this direction. But the main current ran strongly in the direction of more and more economic nationalism,[6] imperialism, and war preparations.

5 J. A. Hobson, *Imperialism,* London, 1902, pp. 53–54.

6 In Great Britain, for the historical reasons

The plutocracy, in short, showed no inclination to behave in the way German Social-Democrats had proved they must, and Norman Angellites argued they ought to, behave out of enlightened self-interest. They remained obstinately unenlightened, short-sighted, and selfish. Why this was, still is, and will probably remain the case until the plutocracy are literally put out of

touched on in the last chapter, free trade survived almost intact until the great slump. But absence of tariff discrimination, either in British or any other colonies, never meant effective equality of opportunity in investment, road, rail and engineering contracts, etc. With unimportant exceptions the bulk of the trade and almost all the loans and development projects in colonies have always been in the hands of nationals of the power having sovereignty over those colonies. This is a hard fact to which Norman Angellites are apt to pay too little attention.

business need not be discussed at this juncture. It is enough to point out that this was so, and that the fact was of decisive importance in stultifying democracy and plunging the world into World War I.

. . . . . .

If there is one lesson that stands out above all the others to be learned from the history of how World War I came, how the war ended, and what has happened since, it is the almost unbelievable blindness, tenacity, cruelty, and unscrupulousness with which the governing classes cling to their privileges and power at any cost to their suffering peoples and to the wider interests of peace and civilization. They are so expert and cunning on details, and so blind and foolish on fundamentals.

Background of the War:
General Conclusion

PIERRE RENOUVIN

Professor of contemporary history and Dean of the Faculty of Letters at the Sorbonne, Professor of diplomatic history at the Institut d'Études Politiques, and member of the Institut de France, Pierre Renouvin stands at the peak of the historical profession in France. His major contribution to the controversy over war guilt, *The Immediate Origins of the War*, appeared in France in 1927 and in English translation in 1928. Since then he has ranged widely over the fields of politics and diplomatic history, completing a seven-volume series on the history of international relations of which he has edited the earlier volumes and has himself written the last three on the period since 1815. Though he took an anti-revisionist position in his earlier works, he now presents the better balanced interpretation which emphasizes trends and movements rather than individual or national guilt; and while he recognizes economic and social forces he does not ascribe to them the importance that Zilliacus does. The following extract comes from the concluding pages of Renouvin's sixth volume in the series on international relations. His views here may be compared with those of Taylor, Aron, and Schmitt.

IN SURVEYING the whole of that period [1871–1914], which marked both the apogee of Europe and the first signs of its decline, diplomatic conflicts make sense only when considered within the framework of economic and social changes. The extension and accelerated tempo of industrial development; the rise of finance capitalism; the contrasts among social groups; the vast movements of transatlantic emigration; the spread of primary education; the power of the daily press; and also, not to be forgotten, the extension of military duties and obligations — all these aspects of a transformed world gave to international relations a new character. Consequently we must try to evaluate the respective influence of underlying causes and of diplomatic actions. . . .

With respect to the role of individual initiative, always important in diplomatic action, the "Bismarckian period" offers a contrast to the one that followed it.

How can one study the history of the period prior to 1890 without being struck by the deeds or the aims of that statesman toward whom all the others — Disraeli or Gladstone, Jules Ferry, Gorchakov — constantly looked? In the diplomatic correspondence nothing is more striking than the perpetual presence of the German chancellor or his shadow: What is Bismarck thinking and what is he getting ready to do? . . . "Bismarckism" is a reality of the collective

From: Pierre Renouvin, *Histoire des relations internationales*: VI. Le XIXe Siècle; 2e Partie: De 1871 à 1914 (Paris, 1955), pp. 377–84. (Extracts translated by the editor.) By permission of Librairie Hachette.

psychology and consequently an indispensable explanatory element in the study of that epoch.

After the fall of the Chancellor the picture is quite altered. William II, failing to find "his Bismarck" — and even if he had met him, would he have supported him long? — was forced to push to the front of the stage some inferior actors, or at the very best a brilliant diplomat. Were the other European governments any better served? The epoch is poor in statesmen. On the one hand there is a disturbing levity, that of an Izvolski or a Berchtold, or a mediocrity that failed even to fool people at the time; on the other hand, there is the ordinary propriety of the high-ranking bureaucrat who disposes of the current business without ever looking beyond it; or, again, the confirmed parliamentarian who courts a "diplomatic success" even if this success is ineffectual or dangerous. Undoubtedly some men emerge from this grey monochrome because of striking characteristics: Salisbury's shrewdness and Raymond Poincaré's firmness of spirit, for example. But even among those whose work was most significant and whose program went beyond the customary horizon — Joseph Chamberlain, Delcassé, Aehrenthal — their strength of will and their audacity were more noteworthy than their farsightedness.

Around these ministers, what of those who collaborated with them in determining external policy?

The high diplomatic personnel in all the great states included many men whose professional conscientiousness, perspicacity in gathering political news, and dexterity in negotiation were excellent, and whose advice was taken. But nowhere, especially in France, did the great ambassadors during the twentieth century have enough character and personal authority to become, in grave situations, the counsellors of their governments, and to assume, even sometimes, the role of "mentors." Nowhere, moreover, did diplomatic agents exceed their instructions with more quiet assurance than in the Russian autocracy The study

of that diplomatic world remains indispensable for understanding its political practices, and without a doubt it allows us to catch a glimpse of a socially closed circle which in many cases tended to neglect profound changes and to believe that the aims or the maneuvers of chancelleries are the center of interest in international relations. But that very fact is one element in explaining the history of the time.

High military and naval personnel merit no less attention if we bear in mind the necessary harmony between the determination of external policy and the quality of the armed forces. Note that in the states whose regime was democratic and parliamentary the government, between 1900 and 1914, never stopped supervising the plans of the general staff, perhaps simply because it harbored a secret mistrust of military chiefs; and that, on the other hand, in Germany the general staff was freer in its action and freer to yield to the temptation to profit from a superiority in armaments.

It is nevertheless true that in the development of international "tensions," individual initiative at the beginning of the twentieth century was far from playing a role comparable with that which it had played between 1850 and 1870. One must look at Japan of the Meiji era and at the United States during Theodore Roosevelt's presidency in order to gain a different impression. On the "Old Continent" the actions of the statesman seemed to be dominated by conditions which perhaps he did not perceive clearly, and which he surely was incapable of mastering. Even in the final crisis when, however, certain "choices" taken by the governments seemed to be decisive, can one study these choices without taking account of the underlying forces?

It is therefore the influence of these forces which historical interpretation must try to evaluate.

The new place taken in the world by imperial Germany, the United States, and Japan at the end of the nineteenth and the beginning of the twentieth century is attributable in great part to the increase of population which supplied industry with labor and modified the ratios of military strength among the states. . . .

[But] the demographical situation became an essential factor only to the extent to which it was associated with the development of economic production, with financial power, and with a social structure capable of supplying officers for the armed forces. Russia, though it possessed almost half the population of Europe, was unable in that period to profit from this superiority because its industrial development had been slow, its public finances were at the mercy of foreign competition, and its supply of army officers was inadequate for lack of a sufficiently numerous middle class. . . .

The effect of economic and financial forces was manifested at every turn. It was directed above all by the influence of private interests and by the search for profits; but it also took national interests into consideration to the extent that citizens of the same state, despite the social conflicts that divided them, were conscious of their solidarity in relation to foreigners. These forces have been a powerful factor in the expansion of Europe toward other continents and, consequently, in the jealousies and rivalries which resulted from it, for the competition among the great European states in the conquest of new markets and reserves of raw materials, and for the "control" of land or sea communications has almost constantly weighed upon political relations. They had an essential role, even in Europe, in the development of the war potential and in the relative level of armed forces at the same time that they created between certain great states — especially Germany and England — mistrust and rancor. Germany, when it demanded its "place in the sun," was submitting to pressing economic necessities. This rise of economic power exercised, moreover, an influence on the national psychology or on the psychology of the social classes. In the sentiment of superiority, which has been held by the German people ever since the Bismarckian

era and which began to be displayed in the United States at the end of the nineteenth century, the success gained in the industrial domain played a good part. Finally the attitude of a social group toward questions of external policy has sometimes been determined by economic and class interests.

All these facts corroborate the value of the "economic explanation" of history. But should one neglect the data that correct or limit it?

Rivalries between colonial imperialisms have often reached the critical point where the adversaries seemed to have said their "last word"; and yet these conflicts have not gone beyond threats: the Afghanistan question was regulated in 1885 by an Anglo-Russian compromise; the English cabinet, in spite of the importance of Far Eastern markets for the British economy, left Port Arthur to Russia in 1898; and the French government, as much as it wanted to reopen the "Egyptian question," recoiled at the time of Fashoda before the prospect of an armed conflict. Fundamentally governments and peoples have been conscious that these clashes over material interests were not worth a war, at least a "great war."

Competition between national economies does not seem to have been any more of a determinant. In the tension between France and Germany and in the German-Russian difficulties, economic interests have doubtless had a role, but a secondary one, as far as the present state of research makes it possible to judge. And in the "typical case," the Anglo-German commercial rivalry, what do we see? Did English business circles, even those most directly affected by German competition, dream of combatting this competition by arms? There is no evidence that would let us think so; and the state of mind of the financiers in the City, hostile in 1914 to an armed intervention on the continent, dictates a negative answer. Did the great German industrialists, in order to avoid possible but future dangers, have an interest in making war on Russia, their best European supplier, and on Great Britain, their best customer? Did they need to open up by force of arms any new foreign markets, when the prosperity of their enterprises in 1914 was in no way menaced for the immediate future, and when the perspective had been opened to them of enlarging their outlets in Asia Minor and in Africa by agreements concluded with Great Britain? It must be said that proofs are lacking.

The spiritual and emotional forces had a very unequal influence.

The role of religious feeling, although it was not negligible even in that epoch when rationalism made so much progress, remained nevertheless secondary from the viewpoint of international relations.

. . . . . .

But the vigorous assertion of national feeling is one of the basic traits of the period. There were the protests of "national minorities," subjected to a foreign domination, on the one hand, and, on the other, the growth of nationalisms which did not shrink from invoking the security interests of the state and appealing to traditions or permanent principles, often doubtful or illusory, but which expressed the desire for prestige and the will to power. The nationalistic movement shook the Balkan peninsula, threatened the existence of Austria-Hungary, disturbed Russia and Great Britain. Nationalism asserted itself in the majority of great European states, while it lay at the root of the new Japanese power; national sentiment was finally awakened even in China when European pressure there became too heavy.

In many cases this force took into its service the economic or financial interests which became the instruments of political action instead of being the driving power behind it; tariff and capital investments policies were often adopted by the state for the sake of its desire for power.

Historical explanation cannot be more simple than the behavior of human groups. If it isolates one of the aspects of this behavior, it falsifies it because, between the attraction of material interests and the impulsion of nationalist feelings, the influences are reciprocal. In 1914 the relations among the states would have looked quite different if the economic life of the world had not undergone some profound changes in the course of the preceding half century. But does that mean that the European war was the necessary result of the clash between material interests? In fact, the conflict occurred only at the moment when political considerations — concern for safeguarding security or the desire for power — clashed violently. Without doubt, in these same considerations economic interests might have had a place, for governments and peoples did not ignore the material advantages that success would bring them. But it was not this calculation that guided their acquiescence or their choice of action. The effective impulsion came from national feeling and from passionate emotions.

The Outbreak of War

A. J. P. TAYLOR

One of the outstanding British historians, a Fellow of Magdalen College at Oxford, A. J. P. Taylor has made a name for himself by his facile and provocative studies in nineteenth and twentieth century European history. The extract below from his scintillating treatment of European diplomatic history from 1848 to 1918 represents recent trends toward the reassertion of German responsibility for the First World War and emphasis on the power factor in international relations. His insistence upon Germany's willingness to go to war, his excuse for the Russian mobilization, his interpretation of the balance of power are high points in his exposition which require critical and thoughtful examination before acceptance or rejection.

No Power of the Triple Entente wanted a European upheaval;[1] all three would have liked to turn their backs on Europe and to pursue their imperial expansion in Asia and Africa. Germany, on the other hand, had come to feel that she could expand her overseas empire only after she had destroyed the European Balance of Power; and Austria-Hungary wanted a Balkan war in order to survive at all.

Yet it would be wrong to exaggerate the rigidity of the system of alliances or to regard the European war as inevitable. No war is inevitable until it breaks out. The existing alliances were all precarious. Italy was only the extreme example — renewing the Triple Alliance and making exaggerated promises of military support to Germany on one side; seeking to negotiate a Mediterranean agreement with France and Great Britain on the other. In France the Russian alliance was increasingly unpopular; it was threatened by a coalition between Caillaux the radical and Jaurès the socialist, which in the summer of 1914 seemed inevitable. Both men were anti-Russian, or at least anti-tsarist; both were friendly to Germany. In England the crisis over Home Rule was reaching its height. If it had exploded, there must have followed either a radical government, which would have been friendly to Germany, or — less likely — a conservative government, so weak as to be debarred from having a foreign policy. Moreover, in June 1914, the British government at last reached agreement with Germany over the Bagdad railway; and the French had already done so in February. Both seemed to be taking sides with Germany against Russia in the great question of Turkey-in-Asia. The Russians had every reason to be dissatisfied with their position. The conservatives at court disliked both the estrangement from Germany and

[1] It is often said that the French projected war in order to recover Alsace and Lorraine. There is not a scrap of evidence for this. The French knew that they would be hard put to it to maintain their independence against Germany if it came to a war, let alone make gains. Of course they demanded Alsace and Lorraine when war broke out, just as the British demanded the destruction of the German navy and the Russians demanded Constantinople. But these demands did not cause the war; they were caused by it.

From A. J. P. Taylor, *The Struggle for Mastery in Europe, 1848–1918* (Oxford, 1954), pp. 518–30. Reprinted by permission of The Clarendon Press.

the demagogic patronage of Serbia. Imperialists were offended by British policy in Persia, especially its pursuit of oil-concessions.[2] They would gladly have swung on to an anti-British course, if Germany had given them security at the Straits.[3] Some Russians, more daring still, thought of an alliance with Turkey against the three western "capitalist" Powers; and in May 1914 a Turkish delegation visited Nicholas II at Livadia. If this revival of Unkiar Skelessi had been achieved, a diplomatic revolution must certainly have followed. As it was, alliance between Russia and Turkey had to wait until 1921.

Plenty of Germans knew that the ring round them was not solid. Bethmann and the foreign ministry counted rightly that Great Britain would turn away from Russia and towards them, if France were left alone. The great capitalists were winning the mastery of Europe without war: the industries of southern Russia, the iron-fields of Lorraine and Normandy were already largely under their control. Each group in Germany had a single enemy and would have liked to make peace with the others. But Germany lacked a directing hand to insist on priorities. It was easier to acquiesce in all the aggressive impulses and to drift with events. Germany lay in the centre of Europe. She could use this position to play off her neighbours against each other, as Bismarck had done and as Hitler was to do; or she could abuse her position to unite her neighbours against her, not from policy, but by having none. Tirpitz and his capitalist supporters wanted a naval conflict with Great Britain and deplored the hostility to France and Russia; the professional soldiers and their capitalist supporters wanted a continental war, especially against France, and deplored the naval rivalry with Great Britain; the mass parties — the social democrats and the Roman Catholic Centre — were friendly to both Great Britain and France and could be won only for the old radical programme of war against Russia. It is futile to discuss whether the great navy, the Bagdad railway, or the bid for continental supremacy was the decisive factor in German policy. But the bid for continental supremacy was certainly decisive in bringing on the European war. If Germany destroyed France as an independent Power, she could then pursue her imperial rivalries against Russia and Great Britain with some chance of success. Both Powers had recognized this by supporting the independence of France long before either the German navy or the Bagdad railway existed. Nevertheless, they would not have been so ready to co-operate with France, and not ready at all to co-operate with each other, if Germany had not also challenged them directly. German policy, or rather lack of it, made the Triple Entente a reality. The feeble rulers of Germany, William II and Bethmann, preferred a ring of foreign enemies to trouble at home.

It has been strongly argued that the Germans deliberately timed war for August 1914.[4] There is little evidence for this, and a decisive argument against it. Bethmann and William II were incapable of consistent policy; Moltke, the chief-of-staff, could not conduct a campaign, let alone make a war. The Germans were involved in war by Austria-Hungary, but they went with her willingly. It was easy to co-operate with her; it would have needed a statesman to refuse. On 28 June Francis Ferdinand was assassinated at Sarejevo, the capital of Bosnia, by a Bosnian Serb.[5] Berchtold was

[2] In the spring of 1914 the Anglo-Persian Oil company, which was controlled by the Admiralty, made a compact with German interests in order to exclude their Russian and American competitors.

[3] This was always Nicolson's fear, and also that of Buchanan, ambassador at St. Petersburg. "Russia may strike a bargain with Germany and then resume her liberty of action in Turkey and Persia. Our position then would be a parlous one." Buchanan to Nicolson, 26 Apr. 1914. [Gooch and Temperley, eds.,] *British Documents*, x(ii), no. 588.

[4] For instance by R. C. K. Ensor, *England 1870–1914*, pp. 469–70, 482.

[5] Much ink has been spilled over the question whether the Serbian government knew of the plot. A certain Ljuba Jovanovich claimed to have

weary of being jeered at by Conrad as irresolute and feeble. Moreover, when Turkey-in-Asia took the place of the Balkans as the centre of international rivalry, Austria-Hungary was pushed aside too; and the Germans had rejected with impatience Berchtold's claim to be allotted a 'sphere' in Asia Minor.[6] The murder at Sarejevo revived the Balkan question and enabled Austria-Hungary to reappear misleadingly as a Great Power. This time she could only hold the centre of the stage if she actually provoked a war. The German talk of writing off Austria-Hungary and of somehow restoring good relations with Russia at her expense had not escaped Austrian attention: and the Habsburg monarchy brought on its mortal crisis to prove that it was still alive.

Berchtold determined to force war on Serbia, though he had no proofs of Serbian complicity and never found any.[7] Tisza, the Hungarian prime minister, opposed him. Berchtold wanted to restore the prestige of the monarchy; Tisza cared only for great Hungary. Like Kossuth before him, he looked to Germany, not to Vienna, as Hungary's ally and would not have much regretted the collapse of the Dual Monarchy, so long as great Hungary survived.[8] Berchtold turned Tisza's opposition by appealing to Germany for support; Tisza could not hold out if Berlin, not Vienna, urged war. Berchtold took out his memorandum of 24 June, which had urged

alliance with Bulgaria; added a postscript blaming Serbia for the assassination; and accompanied this with a letter from Francis Joseph to William II, which managed to blame Russian Panslavism as well. The conclusion: "Serbia must be eliminated as a political factor in the Balkans . . . friendly settlement is no longer to be thought of." These two documents were presented to William II on 5 July.

At Berlin there was no serious consultation. William II invited the Austro-Hungarian ambassador to lunch at Potsdam. At first he said that he must wait for Bethmann's opinion; then changed his mind after lunch and committed himself. Szögyény, the Austrian ambassador, reported: "Action against Serbia should not be delayed. . . . Even if it should come to a war between Austria and Russia, we could be convinced that Germany would stand by our side with her accustomed faithfulness as an ally."[9] Bethmann arrived in the afternoon, went for a walk in the park with William II, and approved of what he had said. The next day he gave Szögyény official confirmation: "Austria must judge what is to be done to clear up her relations with Serbia; but whatever Austria's decision, she could.count with certainty upon it, that Germany will stand behind her as an ally."[10] Berchtold's plan of partitioning Serbia with Bulgaria was explained to Bethmann. He approved of it and added: "If war must break out, better now than in one or two years' time when the Entente will be stronger."

William II and Bethmann did more than give Austria-Hungary a free hand; they encouraged her to start a war against Serbia and to risk the greater consequences. They had grown used to Berchtold's irresolution during the Balkan wars and were determined not to be blamed for it. The most probable outcome of all the stir, they

---

been told of it by Pashich, the Serb prime minister, in May. . . . But, of course, the visit was meant to provoke nationalist feeling or, rather, to challenge it. It was deliberately timed for Serbia's national day, the anniversary of Kossovo. If a British royalty had visited Dublin on St. Patrick's day at the height of the Troubles, he, too, might have expected to be shot at.

[6] Jagow to Tschirschky, 25 Jan. 1914. *Grosse Politik*, xxxvii (ii), no. 15100.

[7] This is agreed by all authorities. The later evidence of Serbian complicity, even if accepted, is therefore irrelevant to the judgement of Berchtold's policy.

[8] Tisza also disliked Francis Ferdinand personally, for his favouring the South Slavs and Rumanians. He said on the news of his death: "The Lord God has willed it so, and we must be grateful to the Lord God for everything."

[9] Szögyény to Berchtold, 5 July 1914. *Österreich-Ungarns Aussenpolitik*, viii, no. 10058.

[10] Szögyény to Berchtold, 6 July 1914. *Österreich-Ungarns Aussenpolitik*, viii, no. 10076.

expected, would be an Austro-Hungarian alliance with Bulgaria. Further, both of them thought that Russia was not ready for war and that she would allow the humiliation of Serbia after some ineffective protest; then their position would be all the stronger to strike a bargain with Russia later. On the other hand, if it came to war, they were confident of winning it now and less confident of winning it later. They did not decide on war; but they did decide on 5 July to use their superior power either to win a war or to achieve a striking success. Bethmann had always said that Germany and Great Britain should co-operate to keep the peace. If he had wanted a peaceful solution of the present crisis, he would have approached the British at once. Instead he did nothing. He did not wish to alarm them. His aim, so far as he had one, was to keep them neutral in a continental war, not to enlist their support for a general peace.

The German reply gave Berchtold what he wanted: it enabled him to convert Tisza. He could now argue that Germany was urging them to war. On 14 July Tisza gave way: great Hungary had to keep German favour. He laid down one condition: Austria-Hungary should not acquire any Serbian territory. Though Berchtold accepted this condition, he meant to cheat Tisza, once Serbia had been crushed: her southern territories would be partitioned between Albania and Bulgaria, and the rest would become a dependency of the monarchy, even if it were not directly annexed.[11] The one chance of success for Austria-Hungary would have been rapid action. Instead Berchtold dawdled, in the usual Viennese fashion. The ultimatum to Serbia was sent on 23 July, when all Europe had forgotten its first indignation at the archduke's murder. The Serbs replied on 25 July, accepting Berchtold's conditions much

more nearly than had been expected. It made no difference. The Austrians were determined on war; and the Germans encouraged them to action. On 28 July Austria-Hungary declared war on Serbia. Military reasons were not the motive: the Austro-Hungarian army could not be ready even against Serbia until 12 August. But, as Berchtold said: "the diplomatic situation will not last as long as that." He needed a declaration of war in order to reject all attempts at mediation or a peaceful solution: they had now been "outstripped by events."

The Austro-Hungarian declaration of war on Serbia was the decisive act; everything else followed from it. Diplomacy had been silent between the assassination of Francis Ferdinand on 28 June and the Austro-Hungarian note of 23 July; there was nothing it could do until the Austro-Hungarian demands were known. Then the statesmen tried to avert the crisis. The Russians advised Serbia not to resist, but to trust to the Great Powers;[12] Grey offered to mediate between Serbia and Austria-Hungary. But the Russians had repeatedly declared that they would not allow Serbia to be crushed; they could do no other if they were to maintain the buffer of independent Balkan states. Poincaré and Viviani were in St. Petersburg just before the Austro-Hungarian note to Serbia was sent off. They emphasized again French loyalty to the alliance; but there is no evidence that they encouraged Russia to provoke a war, if a peaceful settlement could be found. When Austria-Hungary declared war on Serbia, the Russians attempted to mobilize against her alone, although they had no plans except for total mobilization. They were, in fact, still acting in terms of diplomacy; they were raising their bid, not preparing for war. The Germans now entered the field. They had assured the Austrians that they would keep Russia out of things, and they set out to do so. On 29 July they

---

[11] This plan of partition, never carried out during the First World war, was put into operation by the Germans (many of them Austrian) in 1941, when Bulgaria received Macedonia, and Albania the plain of Kossovo.

[12] Russian council of ministers, 24 July 1914. *Mezhdunarodnye otnosheniya*, third series, v, no. 19

warned Sazonoff that "further continuation of Russian mobilization would force us to mobilize also."[13]

This time the Russians were determined not to retreat; they raised their bid still higher. On 30 July they resolved on general mobilization. This, too, was a diplomatic move; the Russian armies could not be ready for many weeks. But, in Jagow's words, "the German asset was speed." Their only military plan was to defeat France in six weeks and then to turn against Russia before she was fully prepared. Therefore they had to precipitate events and to force a rupture on both Russia and France. William II might still carry on a private telegraphic correspondence with Nicholas II, which was prolonged even after the declaration of war; Bethmann might still seek an impossible diplomatic success. They were both swept aside by the generals; and they had no answer to the military argument that immediate war was necessary for Germany's security. Yet even the generals did not want war; they wanted victory. When Bethmann urged caution at Vienna and Moltke at the same time urged speedier action, Berchtold exclaimed: "What a joke! Who rules at Berlin?" The answer was: nobody. German statesmen and generals alike succumbed to the demands of technique.

On 31 July the Germans took the preliminary step towards general mobilization on their side.[14] From this moment, diplomacy ceased so far as the continental Powers were concerned. The only German concern was to get the war going as soon as possible. On 31 July they demanded from Russia the arrest of all war measures; when this was refused, a declaration of war followed on 1 August. The French were asked for a promise of neutrality in a Russo-German war; if they had agreed, they would also

have been told to surrender their principal fortresses on the frontier, Toul and Verdun, as pledge of their neutrality. Viviani merely replied: "France will act in accordance with her interests." The Germans had no plausible excuse for war against France. They therefore trumped up some false stories of French violation of German territory; and with these decked out a declaration of war on 3 August.

Negotiations between Germany and Great Britain were more prolonged. Their object, on the German side, was to secure British neutrality, not to avert a continental war. All along, Bethmann had urged Berchtold to appear conciliatory in order to impress the British, not in order to find a compromise. On 29 July he offered not to annex any French territory if Great Britain remained neutral; the offer did not extend to the French colonies. As well, Germany would respect the integrity of Belgium after the war, provided that "she did not take sides against Germany."[15] Grey stuck to his line of policy to the end. He made repeated attempts to settle the original Austro-Serb dispute by negotiation; later he tried to assemble a conference of the Great Powers. He warned the Germans not to count on British neutrality; equally he warned the French and Russians not to count on her support.

It is sometimes said that Grey could have averted the war if he had defined his policy one way or the other. This is not so. The German general staff had long planned to invade France through Belgium and would not have been deterred by any British threat. Indeed they had always assumed that Great Britain would enter the war; they did not take her military weight seriously, and naval questions did not interest them. Bethmann had wanted a British declaration of neutrality in order to discourage France and Russia; once it was clear that they would go to war in any case, British policy ceased to interest him. Emo-

---

[13] Bethmann to Pourtalès, 29 July 1914. *Deutsche Dokumente,* p. 342.
[14] The Austrians also decided on general mobilization on 31 July, as the result of German prompting, and before learning of the Russian mobilization.

[15] Goschen to Grey, 29 July 1914. *British Documents,* xi, no. 293.

tionally he deplored the breach with Great Britain; but he did nothing to avert it and, in any case, was impotent to influence the German generals. On the other side, France and Russia decided on war without counting firmly on British support; the French believed that they could defeat Germany, and the Russians could not risk their own diplomatic defeat. A British declaration of neutrality would not have influenced their policy. Besides, Grey was resolved that they should decide their policy without encouragement from him; war must spring from their independent resolve.

. . . . . .

Moreover, Grey supposed that British intervention would not carry much weight. He thought solely of naval action; it seemed impossible to him to send even an expeditionary force to France,[16] and he certainly never imagined military intervention on a continental scale. On 2 August the cabinet authorized him to warn the Germans that their fleet would not be allowed to attack France in the Channel. Even this condition was not decisive; the Germans would have gladly agreed to it, in exchange for British neutrality. But on 3 August they sent an ultimatum to Belgium, demanding free passage to invade France; the British answered on 4 August demanding that Belgian neutrality be respected. Here again Grey has been criticized for not acting earlier; he should, it is said, have made British neutrality conditional on respect for Belgium. It would have made no difference. The German ultimatum to Belgium was drafted on 26 July, that is, even before the Austro-Hungarian declaration of war on Serbia; invasion of Belgium was an essential, indeed the essential, part of their plans. Only a French surrender could have held them from it. If Grey had acted earlier he would have achieved nothing, except perhaps the break-up of the liberal government; if he

[16] So he told Benckendorff on 2 Aug. (to Sazonov, 2 Aug. 1914. *Mezhdunarodnye otnosheniya*, 3rd series, v, no. 456) and Cambon on 4 Aug. (to Doumergue, 4 Aug. 1914. *Documents diplomatiques français*, 3rd series, xi, no. 754).

had delayed longer he would not have saved Belgium and he would have lost the inestimable value of moral superiority.

On 4 August the long Bismarckian peace ended. It had lasted more than a generation. Men had come to regard peace as normal; when it ended, they looked for some profound cause. Yet the immediate cause was a good deal simpler than on other occasions. Where, for instance, lay the precise responsibility for the Crimean war, and when did that war become inevitable? In 1914 there could be no doubt. Austria-Hungary had failed to solve her national problems. She blamed Serbia for the South Slav discontent; it would be far truer to say that this discontent involved Serbia, against her will, in Habsburg affairs. In July 1914 the Habsburg statesmen took the easy course of violence against Serbia, as their predecessors had taken it (though with more justification) against Sardinia in 1859. Berchtold launched war in 1914, as consciously as Buol launched it in 1859 or Gramont in 1870. There was this difference. Buol counted on support from Prussia and Great Britain; Gramont on support from Austria-Hungary. They were wrong. Berchtold counted rightly on support from Germany; he would not have persisted in a resolute line if it had not been for the repeated encouragements which came from Berlin. The Germans did not fix on war for August 1914, but they welcomed it when the occasion offered. They could win it now; they were more doubtful later. Hence they surrendered easily to the dictates of a military time-table. Austria-Hungary was growing weaker; Germany believed herself at the height of her strength. They decided on war from opposite motives; and the two decisions together caused a general European war.

The Powers of the Triple Entente all entered the war to defend themselves. The Russians fought to preserve the free passage of the Straits, on which their economic life depended; France for the sake of the Triple Entente, which she believed, rightly, alone guaranteed her survival as a Great Power.

The British fought for the independence of sovereign states and, more remotely, to prevent a German domination of the Continent. It is sometimes said that the war was caused by the system of alliances or, more vaguely, by the Balance of Power. This is a generalization without reality. None of the Powers acted according to the letter of their commitments, though no doubt they might have done so if they had not anticipated them. Germany was pledged to go to war if Russia attacked Austria-Hungary. Instead, she declared war before Russia took any action; and Austria-Hungary only broke with Russia, grudgingly enough, a week afterwards. France was pledged to attack Germany, if the latter attacked Russia. Instead she was faced with a German demand for unconditional neutrality and would have had to accept war even had there been no Franco-Russian alliance, unless she was prepared to abdicate as a Great Power. Great Britain had a moral obligation to stand by France and a rather stronger one to defend her Channel coast. But she went to war for the sake of Belgium and would have done so, even if there had been no Anglo-French entente and no exchange of letters between Grey and Cambon in November 1912. Only then, the British intervention would have been even less effective than it was.

As to the Balance of Power, it would be truer to say that the war was caused by its breakdown rather than by its existence. There had been a real European Balance in the first decade of the Franco-Russian alliance; and peace had followed from it. The Balance broke down when Russia was weakened by the war with Japan; and Germany got in the habit of trying to get her way by threats. This ended with the Agadir crisis. Russia began to recover her strength, France her nerve. Both insisted on being treated as equals, as they had been in Bismarck's time. The Germans resented this and resolved to end it by war, if they could end it no other way. They feared that the Balance was being re-created. Their fears were exaggerated. Certainly, Russia

would have been a more formidable Power by 1917, if her military plans had been carried through and if she had escaped internal disturbance — two formidable hypotheses. But it is unlikely that the three-year service would have been maintained in France; and, in any case, the Russians might well have used their strength against Great Britain in Asia rather than to attack Germany, if they had been left alone. In fact, peace must have brought Germany the mastery of Europe within a few years. This was prevented by the habit of her diplomacy and, still more, by the mental outlook of her people. They had trained themselves psychologically for aggression.

The German military plans played a vital part. The other Great Powers thought in terms of defending themselves. No Frenchman thought seriously of recovering Alsace and Lorraine; and the struggle of Slav and Teuton in the Balkans was very great nonsense so far as most Russians were concerned. The German generals wanted a decisive victory for its own sake. Though they complained of "encirclement," it was German policy that had created this encirclement. Absurdly enough, the Germans created their own problem when they annexed Alsace and Lorraine in 1871.[17] They wanted an impregnable frontier; and they got one, as was shown in August 1914, when a small German force held its own there against the bulk of the French army. After 1871 the Germans could easily have fought Russia and stood on the defensive in the west; this was indeed the strategical plan of the elder Moltke. It was not a strategy which guaranteed final, decisive, victory; and Schlieffen therefore rejected it. In 1892 he insisted that France must be defeated first; ten years later he drew the further inevitable conclusion that the

[17] This was, of course, also true politically. Though France would have had an interest in maintaining Russia as a Great Power even if she had not lost Alsace and Lorraine, her public opinion would have been less deeply committed; and the Germans would not have assumed that France would inevitably attack them in case they were at war with Russia.

German armies must go through Belgium. If the strategy of the elder Moltke had been adhered to with all its political consequences, it would have been very difficult to persuade French and British opinion to go to the assistance of Russia; instead, it appeared in 1914 that Russia was coming to the assistance of France and even of Great Britain. Schlieffen first created the Franco-Russian alliance; and then ensured that Great Britain would enter the war as well. The Germans complained that the war could not be "localized" in 1914; Schlieffen's strategy prevented it. He would be content with nothing less than total victory; therefore he exposed Germany to total defeat.

There is a deeper explanation still. No one in 1914 took the dangers of war seriously except on a purely military plane. Though all, except a few fighting men, abhorred its bloodshed, none expected a social catastrophe. In the days of Metternich, and even afterwards, statesmen had feared that war would produce "revolution" — and revolutionaries had sometimes advocated it for that very reason. Now they were inclined to think that war would stave off their social and political problems. . . .

The Balkan wars had taught a deceptive lesson. Everyone supposed that decisive battles would be fought at once, and a dictated peace would follow. The Germans expected to take Paris; the French expected to break through in Lorraine. The Russian "steam-roller" would reach Berlin; more important, from the Russian point of view, their armies would cross the Carpathians and take Budapest. Even the Austrians expected to "crush" Serbia. The British expected to destroy the German fleet in an immediate naval engagement and then to establish a close blockade of the German coast; apart from that, they had no military plans, except to applaud the victories of their allies and perhaps to profit from them.

None of these things happened.

Agreement on the Origins of the First World War

FRENCH AND GERMAN HISTORIANS

After the Second World War there was a renewal of the effort that had first been made in the 1930's to reduce the tension between French and Germans by the elimination of one-sided historical interpretations from school textbooks. Two groups of professors, the Germans headed by Professor Ritter and the French headed by Pierre Renouvin, met in 1951 for one session in Paris and a second in Mainz in order to agree upon the views to be expressed in history texts. Although the points of agreement covered the whole period of modern history, only those directly concerned with the origins of the First World War have been reproduced below. The wording of these points makes a noteworthy contrast with the language of the extremists in the war guilt controversy of thirty years before. Compare them, on the one hand, with the extract from Harry Elmer Barnes and, on the other, with the report of the Commission on War Guilt, and note the shifts in interpretation that have been made on both sides.

18. THE DOCUMENTS do not permit attributing a premeditated desire for a European war on the part of any government or people in 1914. Distrust was at a peak and ruling circles were dominated by the idea that war was inevitable. Each one accused the other of aggressive intentions; each accepted the risk of a war and saw its only hope of security in the alliance system and the development of armament.

19. Certain circles of the German General Staff thought the chances of success for Germany were greater in 1914 than they would be in the succeeding years; but one cannot deduce from this that the policy of the German government was determined by these considerations.

b. The great majority of the French and German peoples did not want war, but in Germany, especially in military circles, there was a greater disposition than in France to accept the eventuality of a conflict.

This disposition stemmed from the place which the army held in German society; besides, Germany always felt threatened as a result of its geographic position in the center of Europe, particularly by the alliances between her possible adversaries.

c. The old opinion that Poincaré followed a policy leading to war is no longer accepted, even by German historians. However, the alliance system created in Europe a situation of such a character that Franco-Russian cooperation was felt by the Germans to be a direct danger.

20. The conflict of 1914 between Austria-Hungary and Serbia was the culmination of a long antagonism which had become manifest since the coming to power of Karageorgevitch in 1903. There was a conflict between the conception of the

From: James A. Corbett, "France and Germany Agree — on the Past," *Historical Bulletin,* XXVIII (March, 1955), 158–62. By permission of the St. Louis University Press.

national state and the historic tradition of the multi-national Austro-Hungarian state. The latter felt threatened in its very existence, while Serbia could not give up seeking its national ideal. As the problem of nationalities had not been solved by the government of Vienna within the framework of the Dual Monarchy it became a problem of European importance. Hence, the policy of localizing the war, followed at the beginning of the crisis in July by the governments of Vienna and Berlin, was destined to fail.

21. On the controversial question of the responsibility of the Serbian government in the preparation of the assassination at Sarajevo the Commission agrees that:

a. there is no doubt of the link between the murderers and the Pan-Serbian movement;

b. direct complicity of the Serbian government in the preparation of the assassination has not been proved, although it seems that certain members of this government had knowledge of it.

22. The Austro-Hungarian declaration of war on militarily ill-prepared Serbia was disastrous politically. The government of Vienna had no clear view as to the solution it would bring to the problem after crushing Serbia. The brutal rejection of the Serbian reply — a rejection which aroused astonishment even in Berlin — placed the Central Powers in the wrong before Europe. By resorting to arms the Austro-Hungarian government wished to forestall any diplomatic intervention on the part of the great powers and thus made a peaceful solution of the European crisis extremely difficult.

23a. Russia believed herself obliged in July, 1914, both by tradition and interest, to support Serbia against Austria-Hungary.

b. Although Sazonoff personally feared war he wished to avoid a renewal of the failures Russian policy had suffered in the Balkans in 1909 and 1913, especially since her freedom of decision was limited by internal difficulties in Russia.

c. The Russian government considered the partial mobilization against Austria-Hungary an indispensable means of pressuring the government of Vienna into modifying its policy. If Russia changed from a partial mobilization to a general mobilization, with all the political and military dangers this implied, she did so essentially for technical military reasons. These were invoked by the General Staff and carried greater weight than political considerations.

24a. In July, 1914, the British government sincerely desired the maintenance of peace and, with this in view, multiplied its attempts to mediate.

b. Under no circumstances, however, did it wish to permit Germany to defeat France. Satisfied with the results of the agreements made with Russia in 1907 it wished to avoid reviving Anglo-Russian antagonism on a world-wide scale.

c. Sir Edward Grey did not warn Germany clearly enough and in ample time that England would take the side of France and Russia in case of conflict because of hesitation in the British Cabinet and of its desire not to encourage, by taking prematurely an unequivocal position, an aggressive policy on the part of Russia.

d. Without the German violation of Belgian neutrality Sir Edward Grey would have found it difficult to persuade the British Cabinet and Parliament to intervene immediately in the war.

25. Although conversations on technical questions took place between the English and Belgian general staffs in connection with the first Moroccan crisis, it is beyond doubt that in the years before the war Belgium practiced a policy of strict neutrality.

26. French policy in 1914 was not determined by the desire for a war of revenge against Germany but by that of maintaining the Russian alliance which was considered an indispensable counterweight to German power. This pre-occupation led President Poincaré to promise, on July 23 during his visit to St. Petersburg, that the French government would invoke the treaty of alliance. This declaration meant, in the circumstances of the moment, that France

would enter the war if Germany intervened with arms in an eventual Austro-Russian war.

b. The French government did not advise against Russia's partial mobilization against Austria-Hungary, but, on July 30, it recommended that Russia take no measure which might provoke a German reply. It is true that the Ambassador of France did not carry out completely the instructions of his government.

27. German policy did not aim to provoke a European war in 1914; it depended above all on obligations contracted with Austria-Hungary. To prevent the dissolution of Austria-Hungary which it considered dangerous, the Berlin government gave the government of Vienna assurances which amounted to a "blank check." The German government was dominated by the idea that it would be possible to localize a conflict with Serbia as in 1908–1909. However, it was prepared to run the risk of a European war in case of necessity. Consequently, it neglected to exercise in time a moderating influence on Austrian policy. It was only from July 28 on that Bethmann-Hollweg took steps in this direction. But Moltke, convinced that a European war was inevitable, insisted, on July 30, as head of the German General Staff and for strictly military reasons, on hastening the order for general mobilization in Austria-Hungary.

The general mobilization of Russia, ordered July 30, necessarily obliged the German government to order mobilization. From July 31 on the attitude of Germany was determined, as was that of the other continental powers, by military considerations which gained the upper hand over political considerations. The decisions of the German government proceeded from the firm conviction that France could in no case remain neutral in the event of a Russo-German war and that a war on two fronts

could only be won if it began with a campaign through Belgium in order to encircle and crush the French army quickly.

These military considerations inevitably led everywhere to the issuing of orders for mobilization and, in Germany, in addition to this, to the hastening of the sending of ultimatums and to the delivery of declarations of war.

. . . . . .

30a. Article 231 of the Treaty was considered in Germany as a unilateral avowal of guilt, wrenched from her by constraint, and as such, it raised profound ill-will.

b. Article 231, in the minds of its authors, established the juridical responsibility of Germany for the damage caused by her armies. It did not imply an admission of moral guilt. This notion of moral guilt figured in the resolutions adopted by a Sub-Commission of the Versailles Conference, but they were not retained in the peace treaty.

c. However, the general affirmation of German responsibility, stated in the preamble of the Allied Note of June 16, 1919, and the circumstances accompanying the delivery of the peace terms to the German delegation, reenforced in Germany the impression of moral condemnation.

The Allies could not agree on the amount to be exacted of Germany by way of reparations. The resistance and animosity of the German people against this part of the treaty were kept alive by the lack of precision concerning the reparations payment and the necessity of constantly resuming negotiations on this subject.

On the other hand, the repeated deceptions, due to the insufficiency of German payments, aroused in France likewise a great deal of bitterness, especially since France was expected to make big payments to the United States.

Causes and Responsibilities

RAYMOND ARON

Able editorial writer for the well-known Paris newspaper, *Le Figaro*, and Professor at the Sorbonne and the Institut d'Études Politiques, Raymond Aron is concerned with the analysis of "total war" as it has developed in the twentieth century. His discussion of the origins of the First World War serves both as an introduction to the main body of his study and as a means of pointing out that public opinion is a new element in modern wars. He is in general agreement with Taylor, but like Renouvin emphasizes tensions and national interests. His treatment of the problem, like Schmitt's below, represents the detached and scholarly approach which had succeeded the emotional involvement of the early war-guilt literature.

FREDERICK THE GREAT left to his legal apologists the justification of his conquests after they had taken place. Public opinion played hardly any part in the limited warfare of the eighteenth century; the professional soldiers, recruited from the lower classes of society, felt no need to know why they were fighting. In the twentieth century, the soldier and citizen have become interchangeable; and the general public, believing itself peacefully disposed, demands an accounting from its leaders. To prove the enemy responsible for a war has become each government's duty. On each side, historians and intellectuals strive not so much to maintain the morale of the fighting forces alone as to clear the conscience of the whole nation.

The analysis of the origins of the First World War, originally based upon the need for propaganda between 1914 and 1918, was carried on, even after the Allied victory, by a sort of revolt against what had happened. Middle-class Europe, proud of its civilization and sure of its progressiveness, regarded war as a monstrosity out of another age. The authors of the Treaty of Versailles demanded reparations, invoking not the defeat in arms, which the vanquished Germans (well aware of what they themselves would have done had they been victorious) would have accepted without demur, but the fact of aggression. The study of the causes of the war was inspired not as much by historical curiosity as by that spirit of moral righteousness. Who were the criminals who had plunged Europe into the abyss of violence? What fortuitous elements had revived the horrors of the past?

Historical research yielded inconclusive results. It did not make an end of uncertainties. Inevitably it disappointed both the pacifists and those who sat in judgment.

The historian, concerned to show the causes of an event, puts two questions, both legitimate, but which must be carefully distinguished. First of all, why did war come at that particular time; and, given the situation, who were the men, or what were the circumstances, that precipitated war? Secondly, how was the situation which led to the war created? The first question refers to what are generally called the immediate

From: *The Century of Total War* by Raymond Aron. Copyright 1954 by Raymond Aron, reprinted from Ch. 1 by permission of Doubleday & Company, Inc., and André Deutsch Limited.

causes, the second to what are called the remote origins. Historians attribute to the former more or less importance according to their philosophy and also to the results of their inquiry. If they come to the conclusion that the situation led inevitably to war, the immediate causes obviously lost importance.

In their study of the First World War, historians were deeply interested in the immediate causes. The actual events marshaled themselves in a highly orderly fashion. Before the assassination of the Archduke Francis Ferdinand, Europe was living in a state of preparedness, but no one expected an outbreak from one day to the next. Following the assassination, and especially after the Austrian ultimatum to Serbia, chancelleries and populations alike felt the dread of approaching disaster.

A multitude of books and commentaries have attempted to explain the week that passed between July 23, when Austria dispatched her ultimatum to Serbia, and the thirtieth, the day on which Russian mobilization was decreed. Archives have been exhausted, responsible leaders have published their memoirs, and historians have reconstituted the conversations, negotiations, and interviews that had taken place in Vienna, Berlin, St. Petersburg, and Paris. The very accumulation of documents seemed to result in confusion.

More apparent than real, the confusion is based upon three inter-related questions: What were the actions that rendered war not only possible, but probable, and finally inevitable? Up to what point were those actions morally or politically legitimate? What were the intentions of those responsible for them?

No one denies today, as no one doubted then, that the Austrian ultimatum introduced the possibility not only of war, but of general war. The statesmen at Vienna were aware of that risk, just as the German statesmen had recognized it at the discussions in Berlin at the beginning of July. Russia, who regarded herself as protectress of the European Slavs in the Balkans, would not allow Serbia to be crushed or permit her to be transformed from an independent kingdom into a sort of protectorate of the Dual Monarchy. The ultimatum was a challenge to Russia. All Europe realized that the initiative, heavy with menace, had come from Vienna, and that it would not have been taken without the promise of support given in Berlin.

The Serbian reply was moderate in its terms, though it rejected the proposal that Austrian officials participate in an inquiry. If we add to the ultimatum the refusal to accept Serbia's reply, and then the severance of diplomatic relations and the bombardment of Belgrade, we have a succession of acts for which Austrian diplomacy (and indirectly German diplomacy) may be held responsible. This, then, was the European situation in 1914 which made likely the advent of a general war.

Controversy has centered mainly on the legitimacy of the Austrian policy. To what extent did the conduct of the Serbian Government justify what were exorbitant demands under international law? Whatever particular Serbian officials or private politicians might have had to do with the preparation of the Archduke's assassination, the facts known at the time gave no ground for holding the Belgrade Government responsible, and consequently gave the Vienna Government no authority to make demands incompatible with Serbian sovereignty. For the rest, there is little doubt that the Austrian diplomats neither desired nor expected a simple acceptance of their ultimatum. They wanted to "teach a lesson" to the little country that was disturbing its powerful neighbor by supporting or tolerating the "liberation" propaganda of the European Slavs. The men who had determined at Vienna to "teach the lesson" resolutely accepted the possible consequences, including general war.

Thus the real issue is whether we may consider these consequences to have been possible, probable, or inevitable. There is little likelihood of a unanimous conclusion. The historian may ponder the influence of one event on another but his conclusions can never be final. In the present case, one must at least say that the Central Powers had created conditions which rendered war probable. Would its avoidance have required a miracle, or merely more diplomatic patience and imagination in the opposite camp? Speculations on what *might* have happened are endless.

The same sort of controversy was carried on over the Russian general mobilization, the first in date (though, before it became known, the Austrian mobilization had been decided on). Was not that mobilization politically legitimate as a reply to the first operations against Serbia? The German military leaders themselves regarded the Russian mobilization as different in nature from all the other ones because of the time that it required. When that mobilization took place, had not the die been cast, and were not the general staffs in the different capitals impatient to set going a mechanism which left diplomacy no further room for action?

As long as we consider only the two questions of causality and legitimacy, careful inquiry compels us to qualify, but without fundamentally modifying, the Allied contention. It was the Vienna Cabinet that took the initiatives which all Europe has held to be bellicose. It was that Cabinet which threw down the glove to Serbia, and therefore to Russia; it was that Cabinet which wanted a *succès de prestige*, even at the risk of general war. Germany, in giving Vienna a free hand, shared the responsibility, whatever may have been the secret thoughts of her rulers. Even though it were shown that the Entente, and Russia in particular, was too prompt in taking up the challenge, the burden of guilt in the diplomatic sequence of actions and rejoinders would remain with the "initiators."

But such guilt, positive and limited — diplomatic, so to speak — is incommensurable with that imagined by popular passion. Search was made, not for this or that Minister bent on extirpating the Irredentist propaganda of the European Slavs, but for the men who had knowingly embarked on aggression. They were not discovered or, in any case, they were not discovered in the simple guise of storybook villains.

The search for motives or incentives leads to unending controversies. It is possible on the basis of certain testimony to represent German policy as inspired by the desire to launch as soon as possible a war considered to be inevitable. The proposals of Wilhelm II to the King of the Belgians may be adduced, for example. In certain military quarters it was obviously thought that the reorganization of the Russian Army would not be completed until 1917, and that the French forces were short of machine guns and heavy artillery. Such considerations, reinforcing the confidence of the general staff, must have influenced the generals in the discussions at the beginning of July. But the study of archives has revealed a German policy less sure of itself and less definite in its aim. Berlin accepted general war, but it could not be said that the responsible statesmen deliberately set out to provoke it over the Austro-Serbian dispute. That idea certainly crossed the minds of some persons at some moments, but it did not constantly determine the action of the Chancellor, the Emperor, or the Ambassadors.

In other words, when we search for motives the simple picture of aggressors and victims does not stand up to rigorous analysis.

The French statesmen certainly desired war even less. The Tsar and a good many (but not all) of the Russian leaders were afraid of war, perhaps more out of concern for the regime than for the war itself. But the Allies were determined not to tolerate the Austrians' resorting to force in the Balkans, while Viennese diplomacy was no less determined to use force if necessary to gain a *succès de prestige* at the expense of Serbia. On both sides the will to peace was conditional, not absolute. The European situation in 1914 made the localization of the conflict extremely improbable, but both Berlin and Vienna would have been satisfied to attain the immediate objective without starting a general war.

The European scene was not occupied by "sheep and wolf" states, but by sovereign states equally determined to maintain their power and prestige. In Britain and France there was no equivalent of the Pan-Germans or the romantic theorists of violence. Both countries were inclined to be conservative and to renounce dreams of conquest. The Germany of Wilhelm II, actively expansionist, was more inclined to the call of arms than the middle-class democracies. For all that, the explosion in 1914 was the result of diplomatic failure.

For a century Europe had enjoyed relative stability. Neither the Crimean War nor the Franco-Prussian War became general. With greater effort the Balkan Wars were brought to an end without irreparable injury to the European equilibrium. The "war monster" that had shaken the Continent from 1792 to 1815 had been chained up. It broke loose again in August 1914.

As soon as we leave the narrow limits of our inquiry into the assassination of the Archduke and the Austrian declaration of war, going back before the crisis of June and July 1914, there is no longer any date that can be regarded as marking the origin of the historical situation that produced the First World War. The Franco-German hostility leads us back at least to the Treaty of Frankfurt, the Russo-German hostility at least to the abandonment of the Reinsurance Treaty by the young Emperor Wilhelm II. But rather than retrace a half century of European diplomatic history, our critical inquiry must restrict itself to the formulation of definite questions.

Any student of the crisis was bound to be struck by the rapidity with which an incident involving an individual prince set all Europe ablaze. Why had the situation become so explosive? Why did so many statesmen and common men alike vaguely sense the rising storm?

The replies of the historians, although differing in detail, are on the whole irresistibly simple, disconcerting to those who want to penetrate beyond the superficial facts and root out the deep-seated forces of which the very participants themselves had no knowledge.

In accordance with an unwritten law of European diplomacy, the very fact of Germany's growth in power provoked a grouping of nations to make a stand against her. The course of the war proved abundantly that the Triple Entente had no surplus of strength over the German-Austrian alliance. But the fact that the Entente was necessary for equilibrium does not explain why it was formed. It had not yet been formed at the end of the last century, though the same considerations had already made it necessary. We must therefore remember simply that the grouping of the great European nations into more or less close alliances was something neither novel nor monstrous that required a special explanation or implied the existence of a culprit.

France, once she had surmounted the consequences of defeat, would normally, in accordance with an old tradition, seek support in the East. It may be that the Franco-Russian rapprochement was facilitated or accelerated by the mistakes of the Wilhelmstrasse. But it would have been difficult, in the long run, for Germany to remain very friendly with both Russia and Austria Hungary. In preferring the latter she inevitably brought about a rapprochement between Paris and St. Petersburg. As for Great Britain, she was bound to fear a German victory that would eliminate France as a major power and give the conqueror almost unlimited hegemony over the Continent. British diplomacy would perhaps not have heeded the peril to its own profound interests had not the Second Reich, by building a military fleet, delivered a challenge which the British Empire could not refuse.

For the rest, from the beginning of the century there was a lack of definition in the diplomatic "fronts." Contacts between the courts of Berlin and St. Petersburg were frequent until the eve of the rupture. Wilhelm II tried several times to take advantage of his personal ascendancy over Nicholas II for purposes of high diplomacy. The treaty signed by the two Emperors at Björkö in July 1905, although subsequently rejected by the Tsar's Ministers, must not be forgotten. Until the eve of the catastrophe the relations between London and Berlin, quite apart from dynastic ties, were not those of irreconcilable enemies. As late as 1914 British Ministers had the idea of appeasing German ambitions by negotiating a partition of the Portuguese colonies. In spite of the efforts of French diplomacy, no British Government had entered into any formal engagement: discussions between the general staffs did not interfere with the freedom of decision of the London Cabinet.

The division of the principal nations of Europe into two camps did not necessarily make for war. It only made it inevitable that any conflict involving two great powers would bring general war. From the moment when there was formed in the center of Europe a German empire, industrially foremost in Europe, with a population exceeding that of France by more than fifty per cent, and allied to the Dual Monarchy, a war on the small scale of that of 1870 had become impossible. Neither Russia nor Great Britain would have tolerated a new German victory which would have made of the Reich no longer merely the dominant European state, but a claimant to empire over the Continent.

The two camps were not condemned to mortal combat by any mysterious fatality. The relations between the coalitions had simply deteriorated until clear-sighted observers foresaw the inescapable outcome of armed peace. Who was to blame? The issue has been passionately argued. One side denounced the intolerable manners of Teutonic diplomacy, the demand for Delcassé's dismissal, the spectacular visit to Tangier, the dispatch of a gunboat to Agadir, the annexation of Bosnia-Herzegovina; on the other side it was pointed out that in the course of the half century during which she had been the foremost power on the Continent, Germany had added less to her overseas possessions and profited less by arms or negotiation than weakened France. Germany had made herself intolerable by her brutality, by her arrogance, and by the ambitions of which she was suspected. But under the rules of diplomacy she was not wrong in demanding compensation when France established her protectorate over Morocco. She could not fail to notice that the international conferences were not turning out to her advantage.

The growing tension centered about three principal difficulties: the rivalry between Austria and Russia in the Balkans, the Franco-German conflict over Morocco, and the arms race — on sea between Britain and Germany, and on land between all the powers. The two last causes had produced the situation, the first one kindled the spark.

There are doubtless those who contend that the immediate cause matters little, and that war might have broken out just as easily in 1911 as in 1914. The contention readily suggests itself and is not easily disproven. The fact remains that the Balkan quarrels brought about the actual rupture, just as they had helped to dissolve the pact of conservation which, despite divergent alliances, still united the sovereigns of Russia and Germany. For one thing, the clash between Russia and Austria-Hungary had a diplomatic cause. Repulsed in Asia after her defeat by Japan in 1905, Russia conformed to tradition and redirected her attention and her ambitions to Europe. But, apart from diplomacy, the clash had a deeper cause in the movement of ideas and passions. For two supranational empires still existed in an age of nationalism. The Ottoman Empire had not yet been liquidated, and already diplomats were anxiously anticipating the time when they would have to face the problem of the succession to Austria-Hungary.

Henceforth Viennese diplomacy is more understandable. It was no longer so much a question of avenging the assassination of an Archduke who had favored trialism and whose disappearance pleased many persons in high places. It was a matter of ending once and for all the nationalist propaganda that challenged the existence of Austria-Hungary. Obviously, Russia could not allow the Vienna Government a free hand.

The quarrel between chancelleries interested also the general public in each country. Diplomacy had succeeded in integrating into the Europe which followed the Congress of Vienna a united Germany and a united Italy without a general war. It was unable to perform such a feat again in the twentieth century. The national conflicts in Eastern Europe unleashed a general war.

The inquiry into political responsibility carries with it no authority to banish as criminals either men or nations. But inquiry does clarify the significance and the origins of the war. The immediate occasion and the deeper cause largely coincide; for, as we have seen, the reasons for hostility among the various nations of Europe were manifold. The relative strengths and the relationships of alliance excluded partial conflicts. The rise of Germany, whose hegemony France dreaded and whose navy menaced England, had created an opposition that claimed to be defensive but was denounced by German propaganda as an attempt at encirclement. The two camps alarmed each other, and each tried to soothe its own fears by piling up defensive armaments. The atmosphere grew heavy with multiplied incidents, which spread the conviction of approaching disaster. The explosion finally came in the East, where Russia and Austria were advancing contradictory claims, and where the principle of national sovereignty had ruined the Ottoman Empire and was beginning to undermine the still imposing edifice of the Austro-Hungarian Empire.

The Origins of the First World War

BERNADOTTE E. SCHMITT

Professor Emeritus of Modern History at the University of Chicago, where he held the Andrew MacLeish Distinguished Service chair, and past president of the American Historical Association, Bernadotte E. Schmitt was early identified with the anti-revisionist school. Since the publication of his *Coming of the War, 1914* (1930), he has continued to study the question and has published articles from time to time, taking account of new documentary and secondary materials. The essay below is a presentation which reflects the mature judgment of many years of study and publication. Compare it with the works of Renouvin, Taylor, the "Agreement" of French and German historians, and Aron, rather than with the early postwar interpretations.

THE tragedy at Sarayevo was the culmination of an antagonism between Austria-Hungary and Serbia that had been growing for a generation. In 1859 the Habsburgs had faced the question of Italian unification, and had been driven out of Italy; in 1866 they faced the same problem in Germany, and with the same result. From 1903, when the pro-Austrian king of Serbia, Alexander Obrenovich, was assassinated, they were confronted with the Yugoslav problem. At the beginning of the century, the Yugoslavs were widely disunited in Austria, Hungary, Bosnia, Serbia, Montenegro and Turkey. In the decade before 1914 it became evident that a national movement was gaining headway because of the rather shabby treatment of the Yugoslavs within the Habsburg monarchy, and one of two things seemed likely to happen: either Austria-Hungary must bring the Yugoslavs outside the Monarchy (those in Serbia, Montenegro and Turkey) under Habsburg rule, or the Serbs, the most energetic group among the Yugoslavs and the only one possessing an independent state, would detach their kinsmen from Habsburg rule and establish a unified independent Yugoslav state. If Habsburg experience with the Italians and the Germans provided any guide, the second contingency was the more likely.

Naturally the ruling groups in Austria-Hungary favoured the first course. The military party, led by the chief of the general staff, General Conrad von Hötzendorf, made no secret of its desire for war against Serbia, which would lead to direct annexation of the troublesome little neighbour. The political leadership was more cautious, thinking in terms of a customs union or a change of dynasty, which might be accomplished by diplomacy, but it was just as eager as the soldiers to put an end to Serbian independence and thus extinguish the restlessness of its Yugoslav peoples. The first step in this direction was the annexation of Bosnia-Herzegovina, two provinces with a mixed population of Serbs and Croats which had been under Habs-

From Bernadotte E. Schmitt, *The Origins of the First World War* (The Historical Association, Pamphlet, General Series Number 39. London, 1958), pp. 13–14, 15–16, 17–18, 19–25, and 26. By permission of the Historical Association. Copies of the pamphlet may still be obtained from the Association, or its agent in New York: Humanities Press, Inc., 303 Fourth Avenue, New York, 10.

burg administration since 1878 but were nominally still parts of the Ottoman Empire. This action precipitated a six months' crisis (October 1908–March 1909), which almost ended in an Austrian attack on Serbia and was settled only after Germany had sent a near-ultimatum to Russia requiring the cabinet of St. Petersburg to recognize the annexation without reference to a European conference. The Russian foreign minister of the time, Izvolsky, accused his Austro-Hungarian opposite number, Aehrenthal, of tricking him, and he bitterly resented the intervention of Germany at the last minute. The echoes of this conflict had not died away in 1914. . . .

The full circumstances of the crime at Sarayevo have never been cleared up. That the conspirators were fitted out with arms in Belgrade and secretly passed across the frontier into Bosnia became known in 1914 and was used by the Austro-Hungarian government as justification for the demands made on Serbia. But precisely who inspired the crime,[1] how much the Serbian government knew about the plot in advance, what steps it took to prevent the crime's execution — either by warning Vienna or by attempting to stop the assassins from crossing into Bosnia, whether also the authorities in Sarayevo took proper precautions to protect the heir to the throne, are questions to which precise answers are still not possible. Actually the answers do not really matter, for an official sent from Vienna to Sarayevo reported that the responsibility of the Serbian government was not established; yet Austro-Hungarian policy could hardly have been more drastic if Serbian official complicity had been proved.

The situation in 1914 cannot, however, be judged exclusively in terms of Austro-Serbian relations, for Serbia, a small nation of 5,000,000 people, occupied a key position in Europe. Romania was the ally of Austria-Hungary; Bulgaria was anxious to

[1] The person most often credited was the chief of the intelligence section of the Serbian general staff, Colonel Dragutin Dimitriyevich, but the evidence is not conclusive.

be taken into the Triple Alliance; in Turkey German influence was stronger than that of any other power. If Serbia were brought under Austrian control, then German-Austrian influence would prevail from Berlin to Bagdad. If, on the other hand, Serbia were maintained as an independent state, a wedge would be driven into the German - Austrian - Turkish combination, and Constantinople would be susceptible to Russian, French and British pressure. So the crisis of July 1914 was concerned with more than the question whether, as Austria-Hungary demanded, Austrian officials should go into Serbia and investigate the *minutiæ* of the crime at Sarayevo. The fundamental issue was a test of strength between the Triple Alliance and the Triple Entente, the outcome of which would affect the balance of power in Europe for an incalculable time to come. . . .

The Austro-Hungarian government quickly decided that the heaven-sent opportunity for a reckoning with Serbia should not be lost. But since action against Serbia was likely to bring about the intervention of Russia, it was essential for the cabinet of Vienna to know what Germany would do in such a situation. To be sure, the German general staff had declared in 1909, during the Bosnian crisis, that Russian intervention on behalf of Serbia would cause Germany to mobilize, which, in German terminology, was the prelude to war. But, during the crisis of the Balkan wars of 1912–1913, the German government had consistently restrained the war party in Vienna, and furthermore, the German Emperor, William II, was supposed to entertain considerable partiality for Serbia. In order to discover the state of mind of Berlin, the Austro-Hungarian foreign minister, Count Berchtold, sent both an official note and a private emissary to the German capital; also Francis Joseph wrote a letter to William II. The letter stated that Austria-Hungary must aim at "the isolation and diminution of Serbia," which must be "eliminated as a political factor in the

Balkans." The emissary, Berchtold's *chef de cabinet*, Count Hoyos, explained that the Austrian plan was to "march into Serbia" without any warning and to partition Serbia between the Monarchy, Albania and Bulgaria.

Only two weeks before, the German chancellor, Bethmann Hollweg, had said that in the event of a new crisis arising in the Balkans, "whether . . . it would come to a general European conflagration would depend exclusively on the attitude of Germany and England." But when Hoyos appeared in the German capital on 5 July, this caution was laid aside. The Austrian plan to invade and partition Serbia was cordially received by the German Emperor and the German government, and immediate action was urged on the cabinet of Vienna. Because a royal personage had been murdered, William II professed to believe that Tsar Nicholas II would be loath to go to the help of Serbia, but if he did, Germany was ready to support its ally and to wage war against Russia and France. This decision was not a matter of Germany putting its head into a noose (as is sometimes asserted) and signing away its freedom of action; both emperor and government knew exactly what they were doing. They made their decision on the assumption that Great Britain would remain neutral (in spite of the fact that the German ambassador in London, Prince Lichnowsky, had been reporting for eighteen months that in the event of war between Germany and France, Britain would join France). The general staff was confident that Germany and Austria-Hungary could defeat Russia and France, and, assuming war to be inevitable, it now welcomed the prospect of war, for victory would be easier in 1914 than later, when French and Russian military plans would be nearer completion. Some conservative elements in Germany looked upon war as a good means of dealing with the menace of socialism, which seemed to be steadily increasing. The emperor and the chancellor took their decision without reference to the foreign minister, a cautious man who happened to be away on his honeymoon and who had hitherto worked to restrain Austria, and without any formal consultation of the highest authorities of the German Empire; furthermore, the decision was taken instantly, without reflection. William II and Bethmann accepted the risk of war with unbelievable nonchalance; it was they who put the system of European alliances to the test. Without this German action, it is unlikely that a European war would have broken out in the summer of 1914. . . .

The Austro-Hungarian government could now act. But because of the opposition of the Hungarian premier, Count Tisza, the plan to "march into Serbia" without warning was abandoned. At a ministerial council held on 7 July, in its place a forty-eight hour ultimatum was decided upon which theoretically would provide Serbia with a chance to submit. Actually, seven supposedly unacceptable demands were included, in order to ensure the rejection of the ultimatum and thus pave the way for military action. In the minds of the Austro-Hungarian ministers the treatment to be meted out to Serbia after the war included "rectifications of frontier" for the benefit of the Monarchy, while other parts of its territory were to be apportioned to other Balkan states; what was left might be attached to the Monarchy by a military convention to be signed by a new dynasty. These designs were of course not mentioned when the Austro-Hungarian government assured the other powers that it did not intend to take Serbian territory for itself.

The ultimatum was presented to the Serbian government on 23 July. It contained ten demands, the most important of which required Serbia to admit Austrian officials into Serbia for the suppression of the agitation against the Monarchy and to take action against the persons involved in the murder of Sarayevo. Outside of Austria and Germany, the ultimatum was regarded as a monstrous document which no independent state could accept. To the intense surprise and annoyance of Vienna, the Serbian reply, delivered a few minutes before the expiry of the ultimatum on 25 July, was conciliatory and to a large extent appeared to accept the Austrian demands, as was later stated by both William II and Bethmann Hollweg. Nevertheless, diplomatic relations were broken off, partial mobilization of the Austrian army was ordered, and on 28 July war was declared against Serbia. The military chiefs would have preferred to wait until mobilization had been completed, but insistent German pressure forced immediate action, which began with the bombardment of the Serbian capital on 29 July.

This action precipitated the intervention of Russia. For generations the principal Russian interest in the Near East had been the question of the Straits: how to break through the barrier of the Bosphorus and the Dardanelles and secure free access to the Mediterranean for Russian merchantmen and men-of-war. Although various plans for accomplishing this had been devised since 1798, no plan existed in 1914, for the Russian generals had rejected a suggestion of the foreign minister for seizing the Straits. The other facet of Russia's Near Eastern policy was the defence of the Slav peoples of the Balkans against Turkish misrule or German pressure. Ever since the Bosnian crisis of 1908, Serbia had looked to Russia for help against Austrian action, but Russia was weak after the war against Japan and the abortive revolution of 1905, so successive foreign ministers kept putting off the importunate Serbs with promises for the future. The Russian government probably did not want war in 1914, for its army was still in process of reorganization and revolutionary symptoms were again in evidence, but, this time, it had to help Serbia or see that country be crushed by Austria. The German argument that the Austro-Serbian conflict could be "localized" was completely unrealistic, all the more so since the Austrian assurances of disinterestedness were equivocal. The Russian foreign minister, Sazonov, vainly tried to get the terms

of the Austrian ultimatum modified; at the same time, by ordering partial mobilization, he sought to make clear that if Austria attacked Serbia, Russia would act. This calculation misfired for two reasons. First, the news of the partial Russian mobilization did not deter Vienna and Berlin from the course they had charted. Second, the Russian general staff was aghast (it had not been consulted!) for it had no plan for a partial mobilization, so the generals persuaded first Sazonov and then the Tsar that partial mobilization was impracticable and general mobilization inevitable. The Tsar wavered, giving his consent on 29 July and then withdrawing it; but on 30 July he agreed, and on 31 July the order was published.

Russian general mobilization was ordered in the sure knowledge that it would be followed by German mobilization, which, according to the German view, "meant war." In a sense, then, Russia "willed the war," as the Germans were fond of saying; the Italian historian Albertini thinks that the mobilization was premature, for by 30 July Sir Edward Grey had come forward with an idea that might have led to compromise and peace. But inasmuch as Austria had attacked Serbia and Germany had forbidden even the Russian partial mobilization, Russia, as the Russian government saw it, had to mobilize or abdicate as a great power. The Tsar promised that his armies would not attack so long as negotiations continued — but these assurances seemed as flimsy to Germany as the Austrian assurances about the integrity of Serbia did to Russia.

From the beginning of the crisis precipitated by the Austrian ultimatum to Serbia, Germany had declined to restrain its ally and had urged it to act quickly. But by 28 July, the day on which Austria declared war on Serbia, the German Emperor had had a change of heart. Reversing his attitude of 5 July when he urged immediate action, he now sensed that the conciliatory Serbian reply had removed "every reason for war"; he therefore suggested that Austria should stop with the occupation of Belgrade and offer to negotiate. On the following day it began to seem likely that, contrary to German calculations, Britain would be drawn into the war. So the German government shifted its ground and advised Vienna to accept a British proposal, practically identical with that of William II, that after occupying Belgrade, it should offer to negotiate. Before the Austrian government had replied, rumours of Russian mobilization began to reach Berlin. The chief of the general staff, Moltke, now pressed for war (as is admitted by the two most objective German students of the crisis). On the evening of 30 July he persuaded the chancellor to relax the pressure on Berchtold to accept Grey's proposal, and he himself telegraphed to Conrad urging rejection of this proposal and promising full German support if war resulted. Vienna did as Moltke desired and ordered Austrian general mobilization — before news had been received of the Russian general mobilization.

When the official news of the Russian general mobilization reached Berlin on the morning of 31 July, Moltke, with the help of William II, secured the consent of Bethmann, who had been holding out against the pressure of the generals, to the proclamation of a "state of danger of war," which was the necessary preliminary to formal mobilization, the order for which was issued on the following day, 1 August. Whether, without the intervention of Moltke, Austria would have accepted the British proposal, whether a compromise with Russia could have been worked out, no one can say; but it is clear that the interference of Moltke prevented any last-minute attempt to keep the peace.

Because Germany expected to have to fight a two-front war against Russia and France, the general staff had persuaded itself that the only chance of victory lay in a headlong attack on France that was expected to defeat the French in six weeks, after which the German armies would be transferred to the eastern front to meet the more slowly mobilizing Russians. In 1914 there was no plan for an attack first on Russia and a defensive action against France. Yet in 1914 Germany had no quarrel with France. In order to have an excuse for attacking France, the German general staff had to make the Russian mobilization a *casus belli* and then ask France if it would remain neutral; since France would, because of its alliance with Russia, reply in the negative, Germany would then have justification for war against France. But the Prussian minister of war, Falkenhayn, was of the opinion that Germany could wait for several days before responding to the Russian general mobilization; Moltke, however, was so eager for war that the German government did not wait to see if Grey's efforts for peace might be successful.

Germany declared war on Russia on 1 August, which enabled the Russian government to say that it had been attacked while it was ready and anxious to negotiate. The German action required France, according to the Franco-Russian treaty of alliance, to attack Germany, but the French government, in reply to the German ultimatum, instead of replying that it would march with Russia (as expected and desired by Germany), said that it would consult its interests. This reply did not stop the German armies from invading France, and on 3 August Germany declared war on France, alleging, wrongly, that French planes had bombarded Nuremberg. Thus France also appeared to be the victim of brutal aggression, a circumstance of great value to France in consolidating sentiment at home and winning help abroad.

France played little part in the crisis of 1914. It had no direct interest in Serbia, but it was the ally of Russia, and if it did not support Russia in this crisis, the alliance would be broken and France would be left isolated. It happened that at the moment when the Austrian ultimatum was presented in Belgrade, the president of the Republic, Poincaré, and the president of the council of ministers, Viviani, were paying a state visit to Russia, and they gave the Tsar and his ministers the assurance that France would support Russia in resisting Austria-Hungary and Germany, an assurance that certainly strengthened the determination of Sazonov. During the crisis, the French government advised its ally to do nothing that would provide Germany with an excuse for war, but it did not object to any step taken by Russia. This attitude was firmly supported by all shades of French public opinion, and the government did not feel it necessary to reveal the secret terms of the alliance. It will be noted that both Germany and France supported their allies on an issue — Serbia — not of direct concern to themselves, and thus it was that a quarrel between Austria-Hungary and Serbia became transformed, in the interest of the balance of power, into a general European war.

The role of Great Britain was not easy. The crisis found the Liberal government facing the prospect of civil war in Ireland over the question of Home Rule, which may have helped to convince the German government that Britain would remain neutral. Actually, in view of the European situation, the Irish controversy was adjourned, and both the Irish parties supported the government in its efforts to preserve peace. Grey made various proposals for delay, discussion and compromise, all of which were rejected by Austria-Hungary and Germany.

Britain was urged by Germany to accept the principle that the Austro-Serbian conflict should be localized, in other words, to proclaim its neutrality, and by Russia and France to declare its solidarity with them as the only means of stopping Germany from war. Grey, together with the prime minister, Asquith, and some other members of the cabinet, believed that Russia could not be expected to stand aside and abandon Serbia, and Grey, attaching great importance to British relations with Russia, refused to exert pressure on Russia to do so or to advise Russia against mobilization; they also believed that an Austro-German victory in the approaching struggle would establish a German ascendancy in Europe which would be dangerous for Britain. On the other hand, they could not announce British solidarity with Russia and France because this would have been rejected by the majority of the cabinet and no doubt by both parliament and the country. At the moment, even the limited commitment of 1912 made to France[2] was still secret, as were also the military and naval conversations begun in 1906. Whatever Grey and his group might desire, and they were sure that in its own interests, Britain must range itself with France, the temper of the country, at the beginning of the crisis, was predominantly for abstention from the war that seemed likely. Grey privately told the German ambassador that, in the event of war, Britain would be drawn in, but he apparently did not inform the cabinet that he had done so. It was not until Germany had declared war on Russia and sent an ultimatum to France that a promise was given that Britain would defend the northern coast of France against German attack, and even this was made dependent upon the approval of parliament and could be given only because the Conservative opposition promised to support it. As Germany promised not to attack the French coast, the British promise might never have been put to the test had Germany not violated the neutrality of Belgium.

This changed the situation immediately, for the German action persuaded cabinet, parliament and country of the necessity for Britain to join the war. Grey was later reproached for not making clear to Germany much earlier than he did that the violation of Belgium would be a *casus belli*. This would probably have been useless. The German general staff had only *one* plan for fighting the war, a plan which involved going through Belgium, and Moltke

[2] By a naval agreement, France undertook the defense of the Mediterranean, and England in return assumed the defense of the Channel. Thus, although Sir Edward Grey interpreted the agreement as not a binding engagement to cooperate in war, Britain was morally bound to defend the coast of France. [Editor's Note]

was not alarmed by the prospect of British intervention, which he expected; he was confident that his armies would defeat the French before British help arrived or, if the British did manage to land a small army, that it would be easily beaten. It is quite true, as Germans have often asserted, that for Grey the German violation of Belgium was not the reason for British participation in the war, which he advocated on general grounds, but it is equally true that without the Belgian issue, the British government could probably not have persuaded the British people to accept intervention in the war in August 1914. . . .

From 1871 to 1914 the peace of Europe was maintained by the combination of alliances and armaments. In the crises before 1914 governments did not take the plunge because they were not ready for war, were not assured of support from their allies, or did not consider the issue worth fighting for. In 1914 what was at stake was the balance of power in Europe for an indefinite time ahead, and the governments were nearer ready for war than they had been in any previous crisis. Austria-Hungary and Germany insisted on a military solution of the Serbian problem, and clearly wished to upset the *status quo;* Russia, France and Britain were ready to tolerate a diplomatic humiliation of Serbia but not its military subjugation, and while they were not committed to the *status quo,* they were unwilling to see it altered without their consent. Thus the alliances, which had originally served the cause of peace, when put to the final test, almost mechanically operated to convert a local conflict into a general war.

Likewise the great armaments helped to keep the peace — so long as they were not used. But as soon as one power, in order to reinforce its diplomacy, began to mobilize, its action made military men everywhere jittery, for no general staff was willing to allow a rival to get a start. "Once the dice were set rolling," as the German chancellor said, nothing could stop them.

III. THE GERMAN WAR-GUILT
QUESTION REVIVED

Germany and the Outbreak of War

FRITZ FISCHER

Professor of History at Hamburg University, Fischer's main concern in his book, *Germany's Aims in the First World War*, is to show that Germany was pursuing an aggressive policy, inspired by economic interests and designed to achieve world power. He begins with a chapter on German policy from about 1900 to 1914, then in chapter 2, reprinted below, he examines the July crisis of 1914 before launching into the aims of the war period. In his view there is a continuity in German objectives from 1900 to the Second World War, although the link between the first and second wars is implied rather than spelled out. The English-language text was reduced by the author himself by about a third from the third edition of the German work. As Imanuel Geiss, one of his students, has pointed out, Fischer not only questioned the taboo of German innocence, built up in Germany over five decades, but also broke the monopoly of knowledge that conservative German historians had held by "just picking up Albertini and reading the documents published since 1919." Furthermore his book helped to divert attention from purely diplomatic to economic considerations. How does his treatment of German policy differ from that of Taylor and Schmitt?

IN SPITE OF all the surface calm, the feeling, or conviction, that a great European conflict could not be long postponed had become general in Europe. Germany found herself, as Moltke put it, "in a condition of hopeless isolation which was growing ever more hopeless." Her confidence in the invincibility of her military strength had been deeply shaken by the increases in the French and Russian armies (of which the latter would in 1917 reach its maximum peacetime strength of 2,200,000 men), and the idea of a "preventive war" was acquiring an increasing appeal, especially in military circles. "We are ready, and the sooner it comes, the better for us," said Moltke on June 1, 1914. At about the same time, Moltke asked Jagow to precipitate a preventive war as soon as possible. Jagow refused, but admitted later that he had never wholly excluded the idea of a preventive war and that Moltke's words had influenced him during the crisis of July–August 1914. Another element of danger was the fact that Conservative circles had come, especially since the Reichstag elections of 1912, to regard war as a "tempering of the nation" and calculated to strengthen the Prusso-German state. Bethmann Hollweg, who in December, 1913, had already rejected the suggestion passed on to him by the crown prince,

From Fritz Fischer, *Germany's Aims in the First World War* (New York, 1967), pp. 50–92. Translation copyright © 1967 by W. W. Norton and Company, Inc., and Chatto & Windus, Ltd. The footnotes have been omitted.

and emanating from the pan-Germans, that a *coup d'état* should be carried out against the Social Democrats, spoke out again just six months later against these speculations on the internal political consequences of a war. He told Lerchenfeld, the Bavarian minister, at the beginning of June, 1914, that:

There were still circles in the Reich which looked to war to bring about an improvement, in the conservative sense, of internal conditions in Germany. He thought that the effects would be the exact opposite; a world war, with its incalculable consequences, would greatly increase the power of Social Democracy, because it had preached peace, and would bring down many a throne.

A month later the Chancellor agreed on foreign-political and military grounds to take the risk of a great war, while recognising — unlike the Conservatives — that the war could not be carried on without the co-operation of Social Democracy.

SARAJEVO, THE HOYOS MISSION AND GERMANY'S BLANK CHEQUE

The news of the murder of the heir to the Austro-Hungarian throne evoked indignation and consternation throughout Europe, but there was no feeling that it must inevitably lead to a European crisis. The reactions were mixed in the Monarchy itself. There was genuine mourning; but a close observer could not fail to note that wide circles in the Monarchy felt undisguised relief at the death of the man who meant to put through some sort of trialist or federalist reorganisation of the Monarchy favourable to its Slavonic elements. Besides the Germans and Magyars, who had felt their dominating positions threatened by Franz Ferdinand, and besides the Emperor Franz Joseph, who had never forgiven his nephew his morganatic marriage, there was also a third group in the Monarchy who welcomed the archduke's death, because they saw in it an opportunity to settle accounts once and for all with Serbia by a war in which Germany would be behind them. The spokesman of this group was Baron Conrad von Hötzendorf, Chief of the Austro-Hungarian General Staff.

Although since 1912 Conrad had described the idea of a military reckoning with Serbia as a *va banque* gamble, if it had to be risked without the support of Rumania — on which he had counted confidently in 1905 — and with a stronger Russia, only a few days after the murder he thought that the conflict with Serbia, bad as its prospects were, could no longer be avoided, and immediately the news reached him he told the Austro-Hungarian Foreign Minister, Berchtold, that Austria should mobilise; she should "cut through the knot," or her prestige would be gone for ever and her position among the great powers be irretrievably lost. But even this thruster, when he tried to persuade the hesitant diplomats, Berchtold and his assistant, Forgach, to adopt the military solution, was not willing to risk war without a firm promise of help from Germany. The Emperor was for taking the risk. Tisza, the Hungarian Prime Minister, was more doubtful than Berchtold himself; the political situation was unfavourable, Russia too strong, public opinion unprepared. The final decision thus depended on Germany's attitude. Both the German ambassador in Vienna, von Tschirschky and Zimmermann, the Under-Secretary of State in the Foreign Ministry (Jagow, his chief, was away on his honeymoon) were at first very reserved and counselled moderation.

But this policy of hesitancy was abruptly altered by Wilhelm II, who was outraged that the ambassador should take so much upon himself. By July 4 the Emperor was all for "settling accounts with Serbia." "Tschirschky will be so good as to drop this nonsense. We must finish with the Serbs, *quickly.*" With his famous words "now or never" the Emperor laid down the general course of Germany's policy for the next weeks. From that hour Tschirschky and Zimmermann were among the most decided advocates of a hard policy towards Serbia.

This reversal of attitude came as no surprise to Austria-Hungary. On July 1 the German publicist Victor Naumann, a confidant of the German Foreign Ministry, had been in Vienna and had talked to Count Hoyos, the permanent head of the Austro-Hungarian Foreign Ministry, to whom he had given an illuminating sketch of the mentality then prevailing in leading political circles of Germany. The conversation was afterwards officially described as having been purely private; what made it so important was that Germany's actual behaviour in the July crisis exactly confirmed Naumann's prophecies. The heads of the services thought the Triple Alliance "not strong enough at present," but the adherents of the idea of a preventive war were growing steadily, both in the army and navy, and in the Foreign Ministry. This "idea" was also supported by a second consideration. It was hoped that the Anglo-German settlement in Africa had "made it certain that Britain would not intervene in a European war." Naumann openly counselled military action against Serbia. The Triple Alliance was strong, Britain would be neutral. The Foreign Ministry, as he knew from von Stumm, would certainly not oppose it, and — the fourth favourable factor — the Emperor would not shrink from war, as he had in the Moroccan crises. Moreover, public opinion would force the Foreign Ministry to let things take their course.

On July 4 the Austrian Foreign Ministry had been unofficially informed by Tschirschky, through an *homme de confiance* of the German embassy, that "Germany would support the Monarchy through thick and thin, whatever action it decided to take against Serbia. The sooner Austria-Hungary struck, the better."

Since Conrad's plans for war against Serbia were dependent on Germany's support, the first essential for Vienna was to secure official information on Germany's definitive intentions. Count Hoyos was sent to Berlin to obtain this. On July 5 he handed Szögyény, the Austro-Hungarian ambassador in Berlin, two documents: a memorandum, compiled by Tisza, on the situation of the Monarchy, coupled with a proposal that advantage should be taken of the Serbian question to attach Bulgaria to the Triple Alliance, and a letter in Franz Joseph's own hand to the effect that the only way of saving the Monarchy from being swallowed up in the "Pan-Slav flood" was "to eliminate Serbia, which at present constitutes the corner-stone of pan-Slav policy," as a political power-factor in the Balkans. Szögyény handed the two documents to the Emperor the same day. At first the Emperor evaded taking a decision, but after lunch, to which he had invited Szögyény in the Neues Palais in Potsdam, he authorised him to inform his monarch that Austria-Hungary could "count on Germany's full support" even in the case of "grave European complications"; Germany, "loyal as ever to her ally," would stand by Austria even should the Serbian conflict lead to war between Austria and Russia. Wilhelm even told the ambassador that if Vienna should decide on military action against Serbia, she ought to march at once. He thought that he could himself dispel Austria's anxieties about Rumania's attitude by a personal intervention with King Carol. At the same time he told Szögyény what had been the chief consideration that had made it so easy for him to decide to support Austria-Hungary: "In any case, as things stood today, Russia was not at all ready for war, and would certainly think long before appealing to arms."

This was, as we shall see, one of the basic assumptions of German policy in these weeks: that Russia and France were still militarily weak enough to enable Germany to weather the crisis, however it developed.

When the audience was over, Szögyény was able on the same day to pass this "blank cheque" of the German Emperor to Vienna, and to report that Wilhelm II "would regret it if we (Austria-Hungary) let this present chance, which was so favourable for us, go by without utilising it." The Emperor had indeed made the reservation, which the constitution imposed on him, that he must get the Imperial Chancellor's consent, but he had had no doubt, as he had expressly emphasized, that Bethmann Hollweg "would entirely agree with him."

This was exactly what happened. Bethmann Hollweg and Zimmermann were summoned to Potsdam the same afternoon, and to them the Emperor unfolded the same train of thought as he had to Szögyény; and, as Wilhelm expected, Bethmann Hollweg, who did not yet know the exact text of the Austrian memorandum, agreed completely with his imperial master. The Minister of War, von Falkenhayn, the Adjutant General, von Plessen, the Head of the Military Cabinet, von Lyncker, Captain Zenker of the naval staff, and Admiral von Capelle, representing von Tirpitz, were now successively called into the presence, and the question of "preparatory measures for war" was discussed with them on the evening of the 5th and the following morning, so as "to cover every case" before the Emperor left for Kiel to start his regular North Sea cruise. The question "whether the army was ready for any eventuality" was answered by von Falkenhayn with "a curt affirmative." On July 17 Major-General Count Waldersee, Quartermaster General in the general staff, who was then in the country, wrote to von Jagow in strict confidence: "I can move at a moment's notice. We in the general staff are *ready*; there is nothing more for us to do at this juncture." For the same reason Helmuth Count von Moltke, Chief of the General Staff, who had been informed by von Falkenhayn of the consultation of July 5 and by Lieutenant-Colonel Tappen of the Potsdam decision, found it unnecessary to leave Karlsbad. How strongly the Emperor's decision had been influenced by his faith in the strength of Germany's military forces is shown by what he said on July 6 to Capelle and Lieutenant-General Bertrab of the general staff: France and Russia were not ready for war; he did not believe in a general war, but thought that now the army had been brought up to its present strength, and with Germany's superiority in heavy artillery, he could regard the outcome of a war with confi-

dence (the campaign in the west was expected to last 5–6 weeks). So, too, Waldersee said: "The plans for mobilisation had been duly completed on March 31, 1914; the army was ready, as always."

"In order," as he said himself, "not to alarm world opinion," the Emperor, after making all necessary dispositions, left for his North Sea cruise. He did so in full awareness of the import of the assurances which he had given to Austria. Shortly after, when he was in the company of Krupp von Bohlen and Halbach, with whom he was on terms of intimacy, he assured him that:

He would declare war at once, if Russia mobilised. This time people would see that he was not "falling out." The Emperor's repeated protestations that in this case no one would ever again be able to reproach him with indecision were almost comic to hear.

To understand the Emperor's insistence, we must remember the criticisms of his attitude made by the military during the Morocco crisis of 1911, and the *Alldeutsche* [Pan-German] threat that if he again showed weakness, he would be deposed and replaced by the Crown Prince.

While his imperial master was boarding the train for Kiel, Bethmann Hollweg, with Zimmermann in attendance, formally confirmed to Hoyos and Szögyény the Emperor's decision of the previous day. This gave constitutional cover to the "blank cheque." The Chancellor left it to Austria to take the final decision but, like Wilhelm II, advised her to act at once, without informing Italy and Rumania; and like the Emperor, he justified his course by appeal to the favourable international situation. Szögyény had been prepared for this communication by the Emperor; Hoyos by Zimmermann, with whom he had talked on the 5th. Hoyos had wanted military action against Serbia *sans crier gare,* ["without warning"], and Zimmermann had given him to understand that if Austria acted against Serbia at once, Russia and

France would keep clear of the conflict. Any doubts or hesitations in Austria were removed when, on the 7th, Hoyos brought back Germany's unconditional promise to stand by Austria even if "measures against Serbia [which, Hoyos reported, Germany advised] should bring about the big war." The conditions for Conrad's plan were fulfilled.

A shift in the Hungarian Prime Minister's Austro-Hungarian policy came at a meeting of the Ministerial Council on July 7. All the participants except Tisza, who was still opposed to it, agreed on the necessity of war against Serbia, either by a direct attack without previous warning or by the presentation of an ultimatum with unacceptable demands which would equally lead to war. How strongly the decisions of the Council were influenced by the attitude of the Emperor and the German military is apparent from the answer given to Tisza by the Austrian Prime Minister, Count Stürgkh, who feared that "a policy of hesitation and weakness" would lose Austria Germany's support thereafter. When reporting to Franz Joseph two days later, Berchtold advised the ultimatum procedure, which would avoid "the odium of attacking Serbia without warning, put her in the wrong," and thus make it much easier for Rumania and Britain to preserve "at least [sic] neutrality." That he counted on the possibility of war with France and Russia is shown by the "long debate on the relative forces and the probable course of a European [sic] war" which we know from Hoyos' report and Conrad's notes to have taken place, although it was regarded as "not suitable for minuting."

Tisza, who on July 8 had still objected that an attack by Austria on Serbia would lead to "intervention by Russia and consequently world [sic] war," had, like Franz Joseph, been convinced by Germany's "unconditional attitude" that "the Monarchy had to reach an energetic conclusion." (When Tschirschky reported this, Wilhelm II added "certainly.") On the 14th Tschirschky was able to report that Tisza himself, the one opponent of war with "Serbia,"

had now agreed to a note "which would almost certainly be rejected [doubly underlined by Wilhelm II] and should result in war." So the first decision had been taken. That Germany faced the prospect of a general conflagration with open eyes emerges further from an instruction drafted by Radowitz, a Counsellor in the Foreign Ministry, as early as July 7 and sent by Jagow to Lichnowsky in London on the 14th. Jagow warned the ambassador of the possibility of "general complications"; Germany wished to localise the Austro-Serbian conflict, but not to prevent it. On the contrary, Lichnowsky was instructed to mobilise the British press against Serbia, although he must be careful not to give the impression "that we were egging Austria on to war." This epitomised German policy after the Hoyos mission. When Tschirschky had reported on July 10 that Berchtold was now in favour of "unacceptable demands," but that her "chief care" would now be how to put these demands, the Emperor commented: "They had time enough for that," and further made a suggestion which he thought bound to succeed: "Evacuation of the Sanjak! Then the cat is among the pigeons at once!"

GERMAN PRESSURE ON VIENNA

The mouthpiece in Vienna of Germany's pressure was her ambassador, Tschirschky, who from July 7 onwards was holding almost daily discussions with the Ballhausplatz, on the proposed action against Serbia. Tschirschky also attended the most important conferences between the Austrians, so that Vienna's decisions were taken, literally, under his eyes.

After Austria had made up her mind to solve the Serbian question by war, Tschirschky called on Berchtold on July 8 to give him another message from the Emperor, who wanted it "stated most emphatically that Berlin expected the Monarchy to act against Serbia, and that Germany would not understand it if . . . the present opportunity were allowed to go by . . . without a blow struck."

As Berchtold reported, Tschirschky confirmed Stürgkh's fears that hesitation by the Monarchy would destroy her value as an ally in Germany's eyes. There was an implicit threat in his words when he told Berchtold "that if we compromised or bargained with Serbia, Germany would interpret this as a confession of weakness, which could not be without effect on our position in the Triple Alliance and on Germany's future policy." Tschirschky's influence can already be traced in Berchtold's audience with the Emperor Franz Joseph on July 9, for the Emperor consented to the minister's proposed action on the ground that he feared "that a weak attitude would discredit our position in Germany's eyes."

On July 11 Tschirschky, as he told Jagow in a strictly confidential private letter, "again took the occasion to discuss with Berchtold what action was to be taken against Serbia, chiefly in order to assure the minister once again, emphatically, that speedy action was called for."

The report by Berchtold on his interview with Tschirschky is supplemented and confirmed by a letter of July 12 from Szögyény. If it were possible *a priori* to think that Berchtold had invented his story of Tschirschky's pressure — the archives contain no telegram from Tschirschky confirming it — this suggestion would have to be dismissed in the light of the Emperor's marginal notes and Szögyény's despatch. Szögyény fully confirmed Tschirschky's attitude. Germany, he wrote, Emperor and Chancellor alike, were pressing most vigorously for Austria to take immediate military action against Serbia. Szögyény believed that this "absolute" insistence on war against Serbia was based on the two considerations already mentioned: firstly, that Russia and France "were not yet ready" and, secondly, that Britain

will not at this juncture intervene in a war which breaks out over a Balkan state, *even if this should lead to a conflict with Russia, possibly also France*. . . . Not only have Anglo-German relations so improved that Germany feels that she need no longer fear a directly hostile attitude by Britain, but above all, Britain at this moment is anything but anxious for war, and has no wish whatever to pull the chestnuts out of the fire for Serbia, or in the last instance, for Russia.

Szögyény accordingly summarised his own views and those of Berlin in the following conclusion: "In general, then, it appears from all this that the political constellation is as favourable for us at it could possibly be." On the 13th Tschirschky was able to report: "Minister [Berchtold] is now himself convinced that immediate action called for." Wilhelm II received this communication (which he again underlined doubly) with obvious relief.

The other way in which Germany was exerting pressure on Austria was by insisting that the ultimatum to Serbia should be couched in terms so strong as to make acceptance impossible; here too the Emperor had given the cue on July 6, and here again his lieutenants followed his lead. As early as July 12 Germany was informed of the contents of the Austrian note, and agreed that it should be delivered about July 25, after Poincaré had left Petersburg. "What a pity!" was the Emperor's comment on the lateness of the date.

Yet although Tisza had consented to military action — he expressly emphasized that it was Germany's attitude that had decided him — Vienna was still uncertain how sharp to make her demands on Serbia. The Austrians had decided to make the ultimatum unacceptable, yet when Berchtold talked on July 17 to Prince Stolberg, Counsellor at the German embassy, he spoke as though it was not yet quite certain whether Serbia would not after all accept the ultimatum. Stolberg reported to Bethmann Hollweg that he had had difficulty in concealing his displeasure at this hint that Austria might weaken. His report continued:

If Austria really wants to clear up her relationship with Serbia once and for all, which Tisza himself in his recent speech called "indispensable," then it would pass comprehension why such demands were not being made as would make the breach unavoidable. If the action simply peters out, once again, and ends with a so-called diplomatic success, the belief which is already widely held here that the Monarchy is no longer capable of vigorous action will be dangerously strengthened. The consequences, internal and external, which would result from this, inside Austria and abroad, are obvious.

Jagow expressed the same train of thought the next day in a long private letter to Lichnowsky. He was trying to answer the indirect warning which Grey had had conveyed to Lichnowsky on July 9, that Britain would never take the side of an aggressor, by explaining why Germany thought sharp action by Austria against Serbia indispensable. First, he argued, war against Serbia was the Monarchy's last chance of "political rehabilitation," for the Monarchy already "hardly counted any more as a real great power." "This decline in Austria's power position," he went on, "has also greatly weakened our group of allies"; this was why he did not want, under any circumstances, to stop Austria from acting. He did not want to force a preventive war, but should war come, he would not "jib at the post," since Germany was militarily ready and Russia "fundamentally was not." The struggle between Teuton and Slav was bound to come (a thought which often reappeared in Jagow's utterances at critical junctures during the war); which being so, the present was the best moment for Germany, for "in a few years Russia . . . will be ready. Then she will crush us on land by weight of numbers, and she will have her Baltic fleet and her strategic railways ready. Our group meanwhile is getting steadily weaker."

The argument that Germany was ready while Russia was not yet ready to strike, was especially emphasized by "German industrialists who specialise in armaments manufacture." Beyens, the Belgian ambassador in Berlin, reported that Krupp had assured him that "the Russian artillery was far from being either good or complete, while the German had never been better." The Emperor, Bethmann Hollweg, Jagow and Zimmermann were all con-

vinced of Germany's military superiority; so was the general staff. Count Lerchenfeld, the Bavarian minister in Berlin, reported at the end of July that Moltke had said that "a moment so favourable from the military point of view might never occur again." The reasons given by Lerchenfeld — which, he wrote, were by no means to be dismissed as "gossip between underlings" — were the familiar ones: superiority of German artillery and infantry rifle, insufficient training of the French army owing to the transition from the two to three years' term of service, the harvest in, and the training of the German first-line classes complete. For these reasons the politicians —Jagow, for example — could face the possibility of a European war with confidence: "If the conflict cannot be localised, and Russia attacks Austria-Hungary, this gives the *casus foederis.*"

If we study the documents and the political moves, Jagow's letter of July 18 to Lichnowsky puts Germany's attitude, and also the reasons for it, in a nutshell. It is impossible to speak seriously either of Germany's being "towed along in Austria's wake" or of her being "coerced." From the Emperor's first intervention in the Serbian question on July 4 to July 18, German policy followed an unbroken line, as nothing proves better than the constant assurances by Vienna that Berlin could rely on Austria-Hungary's willingness to fight — that there was "no question" of indecision or hesitation. But Germany's own aims were even plainer: if France proved too weak, militarily and financially, to support Russia, Bethmann Hollweg — so he hinted to Count Roedern, Secretary of State for Alsace-Lorraine and later of the German Treasury, on July 16 — hoped at least to be able to divide France from Russia. Germany did not care so much what happened over Serbia; the central objective of her diplomacy in these weeks was to split the Entente, and this Bethmann Hollweg meant to enforce at any price, with or without war. In any case the Serbian crisis would bring about a re-grouping of continental power relationships, in a sense favourable to Germany and without intervention by Britain. The conflict must be localised, the great powers should "watch without acting," and Germany hoped to bring about a new grouping of forces in both the Balkans and the Mediterranean.

The German government, as Jagow informed Jules Cambon and Bronewski, the French ambassador and Russian chargé d'affaires in Berlin, on July 21, had no official information on Austria's aims or on its note. The Foreign Ministry, however, "entirely agreed that Austria must take advantage of the favourable moment, even at the risk of further complications," but both Jagow and Zimmermann, in obvious displeasure at Austria's weakness, doubted "whether Vienna would nerve herself to act." Zimmermann went so far as to transfer the description of "the sick man of Europe" from Turkey to Austria.

Berchtold confirmed the "nervousness" of the German statesmen. "Already," he wrote, "Berlin is beginning to get nervous." Reports were trickling through that Austria had hesitated too long before acting, and Zimmermann thought that "he had gathered the impression that Vienna, timid and undecided as it always was, was almost sorry"(!) that Germany was not pressing caution and moderation on her. Berchtold was pressing for action now. Conrad was urging "haste," and the Minister of War, Baron von Krobatin, said that "everything was ready for mobilisation." The reason for haste was to prevent Serbia from "smelling a rat" and "herself volunteering compensation, perhaps under pressure from France and Russia." If that happened, then as Germany saw it, Austria-Hungary's reason for war against Serbia would vanish; but with it Germany would lose her minimum objective of a diplomatic victory, a major political success.

THE AUSTRIAN ULTIMATUM TO SERBIA

After prolonged internal argument, the Austro-Hungarian Ministerial Council in Vienna decided on the final text of the ultimatum on July 19 and fixed the 23rd as the day for its delivery; both the Austrians and the Germans thought it prudent to wait until Poincaré and Viviani had left Petersburg, and thus prevent the French and Russians from agreeing immediately on their counter-measures. So active was the part played by Germany in the events of these days, so strong her influence over Austria-Hungary's policy, that Jagow actually had the time of the note's delivery on the 23rd put back an hour in order to make quite sure that the ship carrying the French statesmen had left Petersburg. The text of the note (the substance of which had been communicated to Germany on July 12) was conveyed by Tschirschky to the Foreign Ministry on the 22nd. If, as is often suggested, the Chancellor, Jagow or Zimmermann had found its wording too strong, they had time enough (from the evening of the 22nd to 6 p.m. on the 23rd) to protest against its presentation in that form. On the contrary: as late as July 18 Count Hoyos had reassured Prince Stolberg that the demands contained in the ultimatum "were *really* such as to make it *really* impossible" for the Serbian government to accept them with honour. As late as the 21st July Jagow had again assured Szögyény that Germany would stand behind Austria "unreservedly and with all her power." When he said that it was "vitally necessary" for Germany to know what Austria's plans for Serbia were, this was not out of any qualms about Austria's intentions, but because she wished, as Jagow put it to Tschirschky on the 17th, "to avoid giving any impression that we were wanting to impede Austria's actions, or to prescribe certain limitations or ends to her."

Now Germany waited for the presentation of the ultimatum.

The day before this was due, the purpose of the travelling about, of the "holiday spirit" of the military and political leaders of both Germany and Austria-Hungary, and of the efforts to keep the "Sarajevo spirit" alive, without, as Berchtold said, "making other powers begin thinking about mediation," became very plain. Vienna thought this the best way of keeping the Serbian action isolated. Germany, too, as Schoen, the Bavarian chargé d'affaires, told Munich (while passing on the three chief points of the ultimatum) wanted to make it look as though she was not a party to, or even informed about, what Vienna was doing. This despatch, however, also traced out clearly the line which Germany in fact followed:

In the interest of localising the war, the government will, as soon as the Austrian note has been presented in Belgrade, initiate diplomatic action directed to the great powers. She will point to the absence of the Emperor on his North Sea cruise, and of the Chief of the General Staff and the Prussian Minister of War on holiday, as evidence [sic] that Austria's action has come as a surprise to her as much as to the other powers.

As early as July 21, Bethmann Hollweg and Jagow opened the official moves to localise the conflict with a circular despatch. Even *before* the ultimatum had been presented, Berlin was instructing its embassies in Petersburg, Paris and London to support Austria's action, and was undisguisedly threatening the European powers with a major conflict if the Serbian question were not confined to Serbia and Austria. Austria's attitude, which had not yet been announced (it was only the *Norddeutsche Allgemeine Zeitung's* communiqué of the 19th which revealed to France the possibility of a major conflict), was "regarded as equitable and moderate," and Jagow now brought the whole discussion between Germany and Austria, including the underlying purposes, before the international forum in the following words:

If the Austro-Hungarian government is not going to abdicate for ever as a great power, she has no choice but to enforce acceptance by the Serbian government of her demands by strong pressure and, if necessary, by resort to military measures. The choice of methods must be left to her.

On the 23rd, however, Jagow realised that this despatch was not easy to reconcile with the story that Germany had been "surprised" by Austria's action. A second despatch, drafted by Stumm, was hurriedly sent after the first instructing the ambassadors not to make their *démarches* until the text of the ultimatum had been published: "otherwise the impression might be given that we had foreknowledge of it." The despatch required the great powers to abstain from any intervention in the Austro-Serbian conflict, even threatening "incalculable consequences" if the warning were disregarded. This demand by Germany for a free hand for Austria surprised and displeased Grey, who did not believe that a war could be localised. In Germany, on the other hand, the conviction that Britain would stand aside from a European conflict was so firmly rooted that when Pourtalès, the German ambassador in Petersburg, reported Sazonov having told him that Britain would disapprove deeply of Austria's conduct, the Emperor wrote in the margin: "He's wrong"; and on Sazonov's warning that he must "reckon with Europe" in case of an attack on Serbia he commented: "No! Russia, yes!"

Yet, as innumerable documents show, Germany knew that Russia would never allow Austria-Hungary to act in the Balkans unopposed. She took the risk of war with open eyes. This is confirmed by the preparations taken by Germany when the ultimatum was presented to Serbia. Jagow, for example, asked for the exact itinerary of the imperial yacht, because:

Since we want to localise the conflict between Austria and Serbia, we must not have the world alarmed by His Majesty's returning prematurely; on the other hand, His Majesty must be within reach, in case unpredictable developments should force us to take important decisions, such as mobilisation. His Majesty might perhaps spend the last days of his cruise in the Baltic.

On July 20 the Directors General of the Hapag and the Norddeutscher Lloyd were, on the Emperor's suggestion and with the Chancellor's consent, given warning by Jagow of the impending ultimatum, so that they could take measures for the protection of their vessels in foreign waters. On the same day the Emperor ordered the concentration of the fleet.

Even before that 6 p.m. of July 23, 1914, when Baron Giesl, the Austrian minister in Belgrade, presented the ultimatum, the coming of war was assumed. On July 18 Count Hoyos had "comforted" Prince Stolberg with the assurance "that the demands [contained in the ultimatum] were *really* such as to make it *really* impossible for a state with any self-respect and dignity to accept them."[1]

Thus only unconditional acceptance by Serbia of the ultimatum could have averted war, and on July 22 Vienna asked Berlin how the declaration of war was to be effected, as Austria wanted her own answer to the rejection to consist of the rupture of diplomatic relations and the recall of her minister. She suggested that Germany might transmit the declaration of war. Jagow refused, saying that it would look too much "as though we had been egging Austria on to make war."

THE "NO" TO BRITISH MEDIATION

The publication of the Austro-Hungarian ultimatum to Serbia evoked worldwide consternation except in Germany, where it was, in general, approved. The suspicion was often expressed that Germany was behind Austria's action, or at least privy to it. This suspicion was, as the German documents prove, completely justified, but Zimmermann denied it, as planned, in a telegram sent on the 24th to the German embassies in Paris, London and Petersburg. He asserted that Germany "had exercised no influence on the contents of the note" and had had "no more opportunity than any other power to take up any attitude towards it before its publication." The previous day Jagow had informed the Emperor that Grey had made his first at-

[1] Fischer's italics.

tempt at mediation, suggesting to Lichnowsky that Britain should urge Russia to influence Serbia, and Germany to influence Austria-Hungary. The minutes with which the Emperor studded Lichnowsky's despatch, which Jagow forwarded to him, show what he wanted quite clearly. His pent-up rage vented itself: Britain's "condescending orders" were to be rejected, and so was Grey's proposal that Vienna should retract any "impossible demands." "Am I to do that? Wouldn't think of it! What does he mean by 'impossible'? These fellows [the Serbs] have been intriguing and murdering, and they must be taken down a peg." He gave emphatic backing to the instructions from the Foreign Ministry which Jagow had sent to Lichnowsky "for guidance in your conversations." These show once more the consistency and purposefulness of German policy in July 1914. The ambassador was told that "we did not know what Austria was going to demand, but regarded the question as *an internal affair of Austria-Hungary, in which we had no standing to intervene.*"

As Sazonov had prophesied, the effect of the ultimatum on London was "absolutely annihilating." Lichnowsky reported that Britain believed that Germany, for all her protestations of innocence, was at least "morally an accomplice," and he went on to warn: "If we do not join in the mediation, all faith here in us and in our love of peace will be finally shattered." Germany, however, made no more than a pretence of supporting the vigorous action for mediation now initiated by Britain; indeed, in order to prevent the possibility of mediation, she actually sabotaged the proposals put forward by Britain between July 24 and the declaration of war. Her actions, and her motives, can be clearly followed, day by day, in the despatches.

As early as July 24 Grey, alarmed by the provocative tone of the Austrian note and the shortness of the time limit, again warned Lichnowsky of the danger that "European war *à quatre*" — meaning, said Lichnowsky, Russia, Austria-Hungary, Germany and France — would break out if Austria crossed Serbia's frontiers. At the same time he suggested mediation by the four powers not directly affected — Britain, France, Germany and Italy — in the event of "dangerous tension between Russia and Austria." Jagow, however, passed on Grey's request for an extension of the time limit so late that it reached Vienna only after the ultimatum had expired. Moreover, he passed it on without comment, which in diplomatic parlance was tantamount to asking that it should be rejected.

Grey initiated his second attempt at mediation on July 25 with his old proposal that Berlin should intervene in Vienna to say that it found Serbia's answer satisfactory. Again the proposal was passed on without comment, although on the 25th Lichnowsky sent three urgent messages advising Germany to give Austria "the hint." This is not surprising: the Germans were furious with Berchtold for having received the Russian chargé d'affaires on the 24th. "Quite superfluous," commented the Emperor: "will give an impression of weakness. Austria . . . has . . . taken the step, now it can't be sort of reconsidered retrospectively."

Meanwhile, Petersburg had announced in an official communiqué that it could not remain "uninterested" if Austria annexed Serbian territory. The French and Russian ambassadors gave it as their personal opinions that Grey's proposal for four-power mediation in London was unacceptable, because the first step must be to mediate between Austria-Hungary and Serbia and thus prevent a local war. Germany accepted this latter proposal, not least in order to prevent the "satisfactory line to England" from getting cut, especially at a moment when Britain, France and Russia were not yet working as one; Grey had stressed that he distinguished "sharply" between the Austro-Serbian and the Austro-Russian conflicts and did not wish to interfere in the Austro-Serbian affair. The British proposal thus meant "localising" the

conflict, as Germany wished, and it was accordingly answered affirmatively by Jagow late the same evening. On the 26th, however, Bethmann Hollweg, while not revoking the consent, threatened that Germany would mobilise if the reports of alleged call-up of Russian reservists were confirmed. But the deeper reason for Germany's agreement, and for her policy — again announced by the Emperor — of "localising the conflict" can be found in the documents of the Foreign Ministry and of the Austrian embassy in Berlin. Germany's undoubted object was to thrust Russia far back. Tschirschky had reported on the 24th that Austria wanted "no alteration in the existing power relationships in the Balkans." The Emperor marked this report "weak," and his notes on it reveal what were the objects which Germany was following in the Serbian question: the alteration of the Balkan power relationships, he wrote, "has got to come. Austria must become predominant in the Balkans . . . at Russia's expense." Szögyény confirmed that Germany's policy was to "localise the conflict," but that she was aware that localisation might prove impossible, and was prepared to risk the consequences. "Here," he reported, "it is generally taken for granted that if Serbia rejects our demands, *we shall at once reply by declaring war* and opening military operations. We are advised . . . to confront the world with a *fait accompli.*" [2] On the 25th Giesl left Belgrade; Serbia's answer had thus not been that demanded by Austria. On the same day Franz Joseph signed the order mobilising eight army corps. The 28th was given as the first day of mobilisation. Tisza, too, in an audience with Franz Joseph, gave full support to the German pressure; hesitation would "greatly impair belief in the Monarchy's energy and capacity for action, in the eyes of both friend and foe."

On the 28th Lichnowsky transmitted yet another (the fourth) offer of mediation,

[2] Fischer's italics.

this time from King George V as well as Grey. He reported that "since publication of Austrian demands no one here believes any more in the possibility . . . of localising conflict"; Britain proposed a conference of ambassadors, "Britain and Germany working together, with France and Italy brought in . . . to secure Austria full satisfaction . . . since Serbia would be more easily induced to yield to pressure from the Powers and to submit to their united will, than to Austria's threats." Grey and the Under-Secretaries, Nicolson and Tyrell, saw in this procedure "the only possibility of avoiding general war." "The absolute condition for success of the conference and for maintenance of peace" was, however, "absence of any military dispositions."

If Serbia's territory was violated, Lichnowsky reported, "world war could not be averted." Britain's disapproval of the line being followed by Germany was equally unambiguous. "Localisation of the conflict, as hoped for by Berlin, was quite out of the question, and not to be considered as practical politics." Lichnowsky urgently advised the Foreign Ministry "to let our policy be determined singly and solely by the necessity of sparing the German people a struggle in which it has nothing to gain and everything to lose." In spite of these warnings, when Goschen, the British ambassador in Berlin, officially presented the proposal for a conference, Jagow rejected it. Even before this, Bethmann Hollweg had given a formal refusal in writing, on the ground that Germany "could not bring Austria's dealings with Serbia before a European tribunal." The Chancellor was not prepared to listen to Lichnowsky's representations, nor to follow Britain's change of course (meaning the dropping of the distinction between the Austro-Serbian and Austro-Russian conflicts). His replies to London continued to take, as sole basis, the British proposals for localising the conflict. At the same time, a circular despatch issued by him reaffirmed Germany's attitude that the conflict concerned only Austria-Hungary and Serbia.

The day before, Berchtold had told Austria's representatives to take the same line, and had added that if localisation should prove impossible, Austria-Hungary was reckoning "with gratitude" that Germany "will support us if a struggle against another adversary is forced on us." Again on the 26th, Moltke had drafted a demand to Belgium to allow the passage of German troops in the event of "the imminent war against France and Russia," thereby proving plainly that Germany knew that war between Austria and Russia would immediately produce a continental war. Finally, on the 27th Grey sent an urgent appeal to Berlin to use its influence on Vienna to accept Serbia's answer as satisfactory, for only so could London, on its side, exercise a moderating influence on Petersburg. Lichnowsky reported that if war should after all break out, "it would no longer be possible to count on British sympathy or British support." Grey had said plainly that the key of the situation lay in Berlin; if Berlin was sincere in wanting peace, Austria could be prevented from following "a foolhardy policy." Three hours later Lichnowsky repeated urgently that Grey was convinced that the maintenance of peace depended on Berlin. In London there was a steadily growing impression that "the whole Serbian question was developing into a trial of strength between Triple Alliance and Triple Entente." If Austria-Hungary tried to beat Serbia into submission, Britain, said Lichnowsky, "would most certainly side with France and Russia" (the contents of this telegram were not shown either to Tschirschky or to the Emperor). Reports came in from Russia that Sazonov was being "more conciliatory," trying "to find a bridge . . . to satisfy . . . Austrian demands." Pourtalès reported, however, that the maintenance of the Balkan balance of power was a vital interest of Russia. Rome, too, reported the British proposals for mediation, and von Schoen telegraphed from Paris that France was ready to negotiate. The Quai d'Orsay would probably be ready to use its influence in Petersburg if Germany was prepared "to counsel moderation in Vienna, since Serbia had fulfilled nearly every point."

THE AUSTRO-HUNGARIAN DECLARATION OF WAR ON SERBIA

All these appeals and warnings failed to move Berlin to put any pressure on Vienna to avoid the local conflict. On the contrary, that same day — July 27 — Berchtold, urged thereto by Germany, laid the declaration of war before Franz Joseph for his signature. He explained that, Serbia having answered as she had, the Entente might yet succeed in getting their proposals for mediation adopted "unless a clear situation was created by a declaration of war." Tschirschky reported to Berlin that the declaration of war would go off to Belgrade on July 28, or the 29th at the latest, "chiefly in order to eliminate any possibility of intervention."

This message reveals another feature of German policy in the July crisis. Not only did Germany consistently reject any attempt at mediation not calculated to "localise" the conflict, but while Grey and Sazonov were trying to gain time, Germany was pressing Austria to act quickly. As early as July 14 Vienna had intimated that it wanted to stop short of the irrevocable. In Berchtold's and Franz Joseph's eyes the ultimatum did not necessarily mean war, and Count Mensdorff, the Austrian ambassador in London, seemed not disinclined to accept Grey's offer of mediation. Germany, however, as she had stated *expressis verbis* on July 25, was pressing for a *fait accompli* to prevent other powers from intervening. When it received Tschirschky's report, the Wilhelmstrasse saw its goal achieved. The Chancellor accordingly adopted an attitude of reserve towards British pressure and showed no inclination to put quick and explicit pressure on Austria. It was only shortly before midnight that he passed on to Vienna the telegrams received that afternoon from London.

And before they were passed on Jagow had prepared the ground in another conversation with Szögyény. Again, as on July 18, he explained how Vienna was to interpret Germany's apparent change of course; again he confirmed the consistency and purposefulness of Germany's policy. Szögyény reported that, "in order to avoid any misunderstanding," Jagow had twice emphasised that:

the German government assured Austria in the most binding fashion that it in no way identifies itself with the proposals [sc., the British proposals] which may very shortly be brought to Your Excellency's notice by the German government; it is, on the contrary, *decidedly* opposed to consideration of them, and is only passing them on out of deference to the British request.[3]

The Secretary of State himself was "absolutely against taking account of the British wish." At the same time, however, deference to Britain's wish was given as the pretext for the apparent acceptance. When explaining his point of view Jagow was more explicit still:

The German government's point of view was that it was at the moment of the highest importance to prevent Britain from making common cause with Russia and France. We must therefore avoid any action which might cut the line, which so far had worked so well, between Germany and Britain.

Bethmann Hollweg confirmed Jagow's point of view when passing on to Tschirschky, late on the evening of the 27th, Lichnowsky's telegram on his interview with Grey:

As we have already [sic] rejected one British proposal for a conference, it is not possible for us to refuse this suggestion also *a limine*. If we rejected every attempt at mediation the whole world would hold us responsible for the conflagration and represent us as the real warmongers. *That would also make our position impossible here in Germany, where we have*

[3] Fischer's italics.

got to appear as though the war had been forced on us. Our position is the more difficult because Serbia seems to have given way very extensively. We cannot therefore reject the role of mediator; we have to pass on the British proposal to Vienna for consideration, especially since London and Paris are continuously using their influence on Petersburg.[4]

Bethmann Hollweg's and Jagow's point of view explains why the British telegram was passed on to Vienna so belatedly, and why the last sentence was — characteristically — suppressed: it might conceivably have given the Austrian government another, eleventh hour, chance of escaping out of the German stranglehold: "Also, the whole world here is convinced, and I hear the same from my colleagues, that the key to the situation lies in Berlin, and that if Berlin seriously wants peace, it will prevent Vienna from following a foolhardy policy."

But London was sent the completely untruthful mesage that: "We have immediately initiated mediation in Vienna in the sense desired by Sir Edward Grey."

The duplicity thus shown by the Chancellor in respect of Britain's grave warnings proves that in the night of July 27–8 he was no longer trying to avoid a continental war, but only to manoeuvre Germany into the most favourable position possible. If this aspect of Germany's policy had not emerged clearly enough from the judgment passed on the Anglo-German conversations by Bethmann Hollweg in his commentary when he forwarded Lichnowsky's telegram to Tschirschky, it is made still more plain from the fact that the Chancellor simultaneously forwarded to the Emperor the text of the British offer, with an exposé of Germany's attitude identical with that which had gone to Vienna. Although he wrote that he had "followed the Emperor's orders" in transmitting the British offer, he had in fact distorted the Emperor's intentions in his treatment of Grey's proposal: on returning from his North Sea cruise on the afternoon of July 27 and on reading Bethmann Hollweg's report that Germany

had rejected the conference of ambassadors, Wilhelm had given orders that Grey's next proposal — for direct influence on Vienna—was to be accepted.

It was only on the 28th that the Emperor read Serbia's answer to the ultimatum, although the Serbian chargé d'affaires had handed it to the Foreign Ministry at noon on the 27th. The Emperor's comment confirmed Germany's policy once again: *"But that eliminates any reason for war."* Wilhelm's "halt in Belgrade" was issued independently of Grey's similar proposal. Since, however, he, unlike the Chancellor, was unaware that Austria's declaration of war on Serbia was imminent, he passed this proposal on to Jagow without much urgency. His opinion was: "The few reservations which Serbia has made with respect to certain points can in my opinion surely be cleared up by negotiation." This was the moment dreaded by the Foreign Ministry and by the military, the danger-hour which might see the monarch's weak nerve give way at the last moment, as it had in 1906 and 1911, before the certainty of war. Accordingly, he was now deliberately deceived. There is no other explanation for the fact that the Chancellor passed on this new suggestion too, belatedly, without urgency, and in distorted form. The only condition laid down by the Emperor in his "halt in Belgrade" was that Austria "had to have a guarantee that the promises were carried out." He thought this could be found in a *"temporary occupation of parts of Serbia."* In contradiction to this, Bethmann Hollweg emphasised to Tschirschky that the occupation must be the means of compelling *"complete fulfilment* by the Serbian government of the Austrian demands." But the real falsification of the Emperor's proposals lay in Bethmann Hollweg's express insistence to Tschirschky:

You must most carefully avoid giving any impression that we want *to hold Austria back.* We are concerned only to find a *modus* to enable the realisation of Austria-Hungary's aim *without at the same time unleashing a world*

[4] Fischer's italics.

war, and should this after all prove unavoidable, to improve as far as possible the conditions under which it is to be waged.[5]

"THE WAR GUILT IS RUSSIA'S"

This addendum of July 28 reveals on the one hand the motives behind Germany's actions and on the other the Chancellor's conscious risk of a world war. For he himself explained what he meant by "favourable conditions": Firstly, Russia must be made to appear to blame for the outbreak of war, and secondly, Britain must be kept neutral. Bethmann Hollweg believed himself to have found the key to this problem in the "policy of localisation." As early as July 26 he had expounded Germany's governing ideas very clearly both to the Emperor and to Pourtalès, Lichnowsky and Schoen, in the words: "Since Count Berchtold has assured Russia that Austria is not aiming at any territorial extensions in Serbia . . . the maintenance of European peace depends exclusively on Russia." Germany's attitude must be "calm," for only if attacked could Germany count on British neutrality and carry public opinion at home with her, the chief need being to get the Social Democrats' support for war. From this point on the idea of making "Russia alone responsible for any extension of the conflict and disturbance of the European peace" appears with increasing frequence in the German documents. Jagow tried to influence the attitude of Italy, Rumania and Bulgaria in the event of a conflagration by asserting that both Germany and Britain were continually at pains to "keep the conflict localised" and that only Russia could begin the war.

The Chancellor took up this line of argument again in a memorandum sent by him on July 28, *qua* Prussian Prime Minister, to the Prussian legations at the German Courts. Again he defended Austria's conduct and underlined his policy of localising the conflict. Just as Jagow, for example, writing to Bucharest on July 26, had alluded to the "obvious consequences"

[5] Fischer's italics.

should Russia move against Austria, so Bethmann Hollweg ended his memorandum with the following passage:

Meanwhile should, contrary to our hopes, an intervention by Russia spread the conflagration, then we should be bound under our alliance to support our neighbour with the whole might of the Reich. Only under compulsion would we resort to the sword, but if we did so, it would be in calm assurance that we were guiltless of the sufferings which war might bring to the peoples of Europe. . . . Russia alone must bear the responsibility if a European war breaks out.

Finally, the Chancellor drafted a telegram from the Emperor to the Tsar which reveals more clearly still his intention of saddling Russia with the odium of a "European conflagration." "If," he told the Emperor, "war should come after all, such a telegram would make Russia's guilt glaringly plain."

At 11 a.m. on July 28 Austria presented her declaration of war on Serbia. It was not until the afternoon that Tschirschky appeared with the Emperor's "halt in Belgrade." Berchtold rejected any intervention as too late. At the same time, however, tension had arisen between Vienna and Berlin. On July 27 Jagow had realised that Austria could not begin hostilities "in practice" until August 12. The German government found this delay regrettable, and in his telegram to Tschirschky of July 28, quoted above, Bethmann Hollweg explained the motives of German policy, which was not so much concerned to prevent a European war, as to avoid Austria getting herself saddled, out of weakness and (as Lerchenfeld reported to Munich) political stupidity, with the odium of having herself provoked the war:

The Imperial government is thus put into the extraordinarily difficult position of being exposed during the intervening period to the other Powers' proposals for mediation and conferences, and if it continues to maintain its previous reserve towards such proposals, the odium of having provoked a world war will in the end recoil on it, even in the eyes of the German people. But a successful war on three fronts (viz., in Serbia, Russia and France) cannot be initiated and carried on on such a basis. It is imperative that the responsibility for any extension of the conflict to Powers not directly concerned should under all circumstances fall on Russia alone.

The Chancellor held unwaveringly to his line: "localisation" of the conflict; should this prove impossible, then Russia must be branded as the aggressor, thus to assure Britain's neutrality. The first object was achieved: from the outbreak of the war to the present day, the chief responsibility for it has been ascribed to Russia. The hope of British neutrality was to prove a great illusion.

In spite of all Lichnowsky's warnings, the German government continued to count confidently on British neutrality in a European conflict. It also hoped that neither Italy nor Rumania would be able to intervene actively against Germany. With Austria-Hungary's declaration of war, however, the diplomatic manoeuvrings reached the critical stage when the event would show whether the confident attitude of Germany's diplomacy and the threat of her "gleaming sword" would again tip the balance and secure localisation of the conflict, as in 1908–9. The question whether localisation was possible was raised on the afternoon of July 28, when Conrad asked whether mobilisation was to be carried through against Serbia alone, or also against Russia; for he needed to know which the fronts were to be by the fifth day of mobilisation, or all the troop trains would be sent towards Serbia. The "automatic operation of the war machine" now began to show its effects in Germany, as well as Austria-Hungary. Simultaneously with a call from Szögyény, bringing Conrad's request for pressure on Russia (Berchtold already thought it essential for both Austria and Germany to answer Russia's partial mobilisation by general mobilisation), the Chancellor received a memorandum from the general staff in which Moltke gave a clear and unambiguous analysis of the mechanics of mobilisation and alliances and explained that they must inevitably lead to world war. Moltke emphasised particularly the causal nexus linking Austria's intervention against Serbia via Russian partial mobilisation to Austrian, Russian and German general mobilisations, which would then inevitably draw in France, the first objective of German military strategy. The general staff's appreciation of the military position caused the Foreign Ministry to revise its view of the importance of Russia's partial mobilisation (which the day before Jagow had not regarded as a cause for German mobilisation). Up to this point Bethmann Hollweg had rejected as premature Austria's request for far-reaching military counter-measures, but under this pressure from Moltke and Conrad he addressed Petersburg in almost ultimatum terms, although the day before, Pourtalès had reported Sazonov as entirely ready to come an astonishingly long way to meet Austria's standpoint, which would have made possible some relaxation of the diplomatic tension. It was technically necessary for the military to get a clear picture of Russia's attitude, but Bethmann Hollweg's sharp tone was also clearly in line with the whole of German diplomacy during the July crisis. So long as England remained out – and it was hoped that a declaration of war by Russia would ensure this – the Chancellor was not in the least afraid of putting the Triple Alliance to the test of a European war.

As pendant to his strong attitude towards Russia, Bethmann Hollweg made every effort to appear in British eyes as the ardent searcher after peace. In two further interviews with Falkenhayn and Moltke, in the morning and the late evening of July 29, on each occasion before meeting the British ambassador, he succeeded in getting the proclamation of a state of emergency, for which the Prussian Minister of War was pressing, postponed, arguing that Germany must wait until Russia began general mobilisation; for unless the blame for "the whole shlemozzle" could be pushed on to Russia, it was vain to hope for Britain's neutrality. If, however, Russia were saddled with the war guilt, Britain could not take her side. The generals, nevertheless, although still bound by the imperial "halt!" yet decided to send to the German minister in Brussels the demand (drafted on July 26) to allow the passage of German armies through Belgium.

In his morning conversation with Goschen on this day of July 29 Bethmann Hollweg again emphasised Germany's will for peace, and informed the ambassador in the strictest confidence of the Emperor's note to Vienna (Halt in Belgrade), again trying to give the impression that he was putting the brake on hard in Vienna, which, as we have seen, was in reality far from being the case. In the afternoon the Emperor consulted successively the Chancellor, Bethmann Hollweg, the Minister of War, von Falkenhayn, the Chief of the General Staff, von Moltke, the Head of the Military Cabinet, von Lyncker (4:40 P.M.), Grand Admiral Prince Henry (6:10 P.M.), the Secretary of State for the Navy, von Tirpitz, the Chief of the Naval Staff, von Pohl, and the Head of the Naval Cabinet, von Müller (7:15 P.M.). The conversations seemed to confirm Germany's hopes of British neutrality, for Prince Henry was able to report that George V ("Georgy") would remain neutral. The word of a king which the Emperor accepted, although von Tirpitz had doubts, brought the conversation round to France, Belgium and Holland. The Emperor emphasised that Germany wanted no territorial annexations from France, although his reasons reflected unspoken first war aims: Germany only wanted guarantees which should enable her to "prevent" further wars. Wilhelm built so largely on King George's reported word that (with Tirpitz's strong support) he rejected the proposal made by Bethmann Hollweg (who hoped to make the offer a sort of reward to Britain for her neutrality) for a naval agreement with Britain.

In his evening conversation with von Falkenhayn and von Moltke the Chancellor again insisted that Germany must wait until Russia ordered general mobilisation or attacked Austria. For partial mobilisation did not create a *casus foederis,* it did not necessarily involve war. Germany must wait for total mobilisation, because only thereafter would both German and British public opinion support Germany's attitude in "the imminent war with Russia and France" (as the ultimatum to Belgium had already put it).

Germany concentrated her hopes ever more on getting Britain's promise of neutrality made contractual — as she had already tried to do on the occasion of the Haldane Mission. In the famous conversation between Bethmann Hollweg and Goschen late in the night of July 29–30 the Chancellor tried to pin Britain down by holding out prospects of a general agreement on neutrality. He assured Goschen: "We can assure the British Cabinet — *provided we are certain of their neutrality* — that even in case of a victorious war we shall not seek any territorial advantage in Europe at the expense of France" — a promise which, however, when Goschen raised the point, he refused to extend to France's colonies. Further, he declared himself ready to respect the neutrality and integrity of Holland, provided Germany's enemies would do the same. In speaking of Belgium, however, he betrayed Germany's intention of violating her neutrality by giving only the obscure assurance (which also agreed *verbatim* with the ultimatum) that Belgium's integrity (he did not mention her sovereignty) should not be impaired after the war "provided Belgium does not take sides against us" — provided, that is, Belgium did not resist Germany's illegal violation of her territory.

The British immediately grasped the decisive importance of this conversation. Now, Grey for the first time recognised Germany's intention of drawing the maximum political advantage from the Serbian conflict, even at the risk of European war.

That on top of this Germany proposed to march through Belgium, Bethmann Hollweg had already admitted. Grey called the German offer "infamous." Similarly, Eyre Crowe, his right-hand man in the Foreign Ministry, concluded that Germany had practically made up her mind "to go to war." What had held her back hitherto had only been the fear that Britain would come to the help of France and Belgium. At the same time, however, the interview had revealed Germany's intentions; wrapped up as they had been, they could be recognised simply as the first stages of those German war aims which revealed themselves nakedly soon after the outbreak of the war: French colonies, in continuation of the policy of the second Morocco crisis of 1911; in respect of France herself Germany was binding herself only if Britain should remain neutral in a continental war (when she would make this sacrifice). In that case she would renounce annexations at the expense of France; but the implied converse of this observance was that if Britain entered the war, Germany, if victorious, would claim a free hand to annex French territory. The same reservation had been made also in respect of Belgium. Since Belgium resisted, Germany afterwards claimed a free hand there also; this reservation was already implicit in Bethmann Hollweg's words.

The position had been clarified. Germany had revealed her aims to Britain in the hope that the attempts made by both sides to reach a political settlement would now bear fruit. The conversation also marked the high watermark of Germany's "policy of localisation"; the despatch in which Goschen reported the conversation, the verbal accuracy of which he got the Chancellor to check immediately afterwards, showed no sign of compromise either in tone or in substance. It was only after the British ambassador, who, as he said himself, had hardly been able to repress his astonishment but had raised no objections, had left the room, that Bethmann Hollweg received Lichnowsky's telegram, which had

arrived earlier but had only now been deciphered. Its contents for the first time shook the whole structure of Bethmann Hollweg's diplomacy, the corner-stone of which had been the hope of British neutrality.

THE COLLAPSE OF
BETHMANN HOLLWEG'S POLICY

Lichnowsky reported that Grey had again repeated with extreme earnestness his proposal for four-power mediation, and had emphasised that Britain, as a neutral power, was prepared, if Germany helped her, to mediate between Austria-Hungary on the one side and Serbia and Russia on the other, but that the moment France was drawn into the war, Britain would *not* be able to stand aside. This upset the calculation on the basis of which Germany had urged Austria to take military action against Serbia and believed herself capable of regarding the prospect of European war "with equanimity" in the confident hope that Britain would after all remain neutral if the responsibility for the war were laid on Russia. Now the situation suddenly became threatening. Only three days before Jagow had confidently told Jules Cambon, who thought that Britain would intervene immediately: "You have your information, we have ours; we are certain of British neutrality." The Germans, Bethmann Hollweg most of all, were surprised, even shattered, by Lichnowsky's report, and they grew unsure of themselves. The foundation of their policy during the crisis had collapsed. Britain would not remain neutral if France were "drawn into" the war. The telegram sent to Tschirschky at 3 A.M. on the 30th to inform him of Lichnowsky's message described the new situation:

If, therefore, Austria should reject all mediation, we are faced with a conflagration in which Britain would be against us, Italy and Rumania in all probability not with us. We should be two Great Powers against four. With Britain an enemy, the weight of the operations would fall on Germany. . . . Under these circumstances we must urgently and emphatically suggest to the Vienna cabinet acceptance of mediation under the present honourable conditions. The responsibility falling on us and Austria for the consequences which would ensue in case of refusal would be uncommonly heavy.

Only five minutes later Bethmann Hollweg sent a telegram to Vienna in which he summoned his ally even more energetically to stop "refusing any exchange of views with Russia." "We are prepared," he went on, "to fulfil our duty as allies, but must refuse to allow Vienna to draw us into a world conflagration frivolously and without regard to our advice."

These two documents, composed simultaneously and despatched to Vienna in the small hours, are used, together with Bethmann Hollweg's address to the Prussian Ministry of State on the afternoon of the same July 30, to prove the peaceable nature of Germany's policy and to show the "absolutly desperate efforts" made by Bethmann Hollweg to make Vienna retreat. But the significant thing about them is not so much Bethmann Hollweg's urgent attempt to get Vienna to accept the British proposals as the fact that they find no parallel among the documents of the night of July 29–30 or of July 30 itself. The first despatches to go out after the arrival of the news from London, they are the products of the shock born of the unexpected information about Britain's attitude.

As late as 11:05 P.M. on the 29th Bethmann Hollweg, completely consistently with his previous policy of "localisation," had summoned Russia in almost ultimatum terms "not to provoke any warlike conflict with Austria." At 12:30 A.M. he informed Vienna of Russia's partial mobilisation and added: "To avert a general catastrophe, or" — and this shows clearly the tactics consistently followed by German civilian policy, uninfluenced by the Emperor or the general staff — "*in any case* to put Russia in the wrong, we must urgently wish Vienna to begin and continue conversations [with Russia] in accordance with telegram 174." [6] The deductions drawn by the Chancellor from the "Russian mobilisation" are astonishing, for telegram 174 was that sent by Jagow to Tschirschky on the 28th, which gave Vienna its first information of the British proposals for mediation, but with the characteristic addition: "You must avoid most carefully giving any impression that we want to hold Austria back." Up to the morning of July 30 Berlin had followed its policy of absolutely pressing action on Austria. It was only after 12:30 A.M. that Bethmann Hollweg saw Lichnowsky's report from London; this he sent on to Vienna at 2:55 A.M. with the first urgent warning. This telegram, however, also explains what the German "advice" for the prevention of the "world conflagration" really came to. Austria-Hungary was thus not being at all "tough" (*pace* Gerhard Ritter) or obstinate, nor set on war, and Germany was not being dragged in her wake. Furthermore, Austria-Hungary had involved herself so deeply in the crisis that neither Berchtold nor Tisza thought it possible for her, as a great power, to give way now to German pressure which, moreover, was not applied with the whole weight available to Germany. Moreover, Vienna had, as the discussions went on, grown ever more convinced that the way to strengthen the structure of the Monarchy was by way of a war covered by Germany.

But this is not the only circumstance revealing the exceptional character of the documents; there are also the warnings given in the course of July 30. For the very next documents show plainly that what chiefly concerned Bethmann Hollweg was not so much to save the peace as such as to shift the responsibility and guilt for the war on to Russia. But the essential point was that although the premises of Bethmann Hollweg's policy, his conditions for undertaking war, as laid down by him

[6] Fischer's italics.

on July 5 and 6, had collapsed, he could not steel himself to change his policy, to talk unambiguously to Vienna and to force it to obey him. A declaration to this effect, combined with a threat to leave Austria alone if she disregarded it, could have saved the Reich from the catastrophe of a war waged under conditions which had become so unfavourable. But nothing was done. On the contrary, the old policy was resumed in the course of the 30th.

This emerges clearly from the record of the meeting of the Prussian Ministry of State on July 30, to which Bethmann Hollweg reported on the situation. His main preoccupation was again "to *represent* Russia as the guilty party," and this, he thought, would be most easily achieved if Vienna accepted Germany's suggestion, namely, to assure Petersburg that she meant only to occupy parts of Serbia temporarily, as guarantee for the satisfaction of her demands. But it also emerges clearly why Bethmann Hollweg was still continuing to insist on Russia's "war guilt." Previously his chief motive had been to secure Britain's neutrality — a hope which, he now remarked bitterly, had practically disappeared; the second factor in his "mission" as Chancellor (second to the *rapprochement* with Britain) now came increasingly into the foreground. If the declaration of war came from Russia, he said, there was "nothing to fear" from the Social Democrats. "There will be no question of a general or partial strike, or of sabotage." The British intervention had shifted the emphasis in his motives, no more. This appears plainly in the despatch sent that evening to Vienna and in its cancellation, which also affected indirectly the German move taken in the course of the night.

If [the Chancellor wired to Tschirschky on the evening of July 30] Vienna . . . refuses . . . to give way at all, it will hardly be possible to place the blame on Russia for the outbreak of the European conflagration [not to prevent the war, but to place the blame on Russia]. H.M. has, on the request of the Tsar, undertaken to intervene in Vienna, because he could not refuse without awakening an irrefutable suspicion that we wanted war.

Alluding to Britain's attempts to mediate in Paris and Petersburg, he went on:

If these efforts of Britain's meet with success, while Vienna refuses everything, Vienna will prove that it is set on having a war, into which we are dragged, while Russia remains free of guilt. This puts us in a quite impossible position in the eyes of our own people. We can therefore only urgently recommend Vienna to accept Grey's proposal, which safeguards its position in every way.

The telegram stresses once again the cardinal importance of British neutrality, of Russian war guilt and of national solidarity as the factors governing German policy. Yet Germany's peaceful protestations to Britain were purely tactical, as is made plain by the fate of a telegram from King George to Prince Henry suggesting cooperation between Germany and Britain to save the peace. This telegram arrived just before midnight (11:08 P.M.) on July 30. Vague as was the glimmer of hope which it offered that Britain might remain neutral, it was enough for Bethmann Hollweg to cancel his demand that Vienna should "accept Grey's proposal" only twelve minutes later (11:20 P.M.). At the same time the Chancellor completely lifted such pressure — and it had been weak enough — as he had been putting on Vienna. No proof could be plainer of the tactical nature of Germany's "peace moves." Comparison with the instructions sent to Tschirschky makes this more glaring still. Telegram No. 200 called on Vienna to accept mediation, since otherwise Russia "would bear no blame." Telegram No. 201, sent by Jagow in the same hour, rejected Austria's proposal for a joint *démarche* in Paris and Petersburg on the ground that Germany "could not take the same step again." Telegram No. 202 cancelled telegram No. 200.

Telegram No. 203 explained telegram No. 202, and telegram No. 204 on July 31 demanded Austria's "immediate participation in the war against Russia."

Besides explaining the cancellation telegram by King George's message, Bethmann Hollweg had also drafted, although not yet sent, a military explanation which ran: "I have cancelled execution of instructions in No. 200, because the General Staff has just informed me that military measures by our neighbours, especially in the east, compel speedy decision if we are not to be taken by surprise." This alluded to the military considerations which became more and more prominent on July 30 and acquired great cogency when the news of Russia's partial mobilisation arrived.

THE BEGINNING OF WORLD WAR

That the two demands sent to Vienna — for tactical reasons, and by no means in any "desperate endeavour to save the peace" — to accept the British proposals constitute an isolated episode, a hesitation in view of Britain's attitude, appears more plainly than ever if we turn to the steps initiated by Moltke when the news of Russia's partial mobilisation against Austria-Hungary arrived. As late as July 29, Moltke and Falkenhayn postponed the proclamation of a "state of imminent war," in obedience to the Emperor's orders and out of deference to Bethmann Hollweg's hopes of British neutrality, but on the morning of July 30 all such considerations were swept aside when the Foreign Ministry (presumably Zimmermann) passed on to the general staff the Emperor's marginal notes on Pourtalès' report that Russia had ordered partial mobilisation. Wilhelm's comment on Sazonov's announcement that Russia was "mobilising against Austria" was: "Then I must mobilise too," and he went on: "Then he [sc., Tsar Nicholas II] is taking on himself the guilt" (for a European war). . . . "I regard my attempted mediation as having failed." In such theatrical wise did Wilhelm II lay down what on another occasion he called his "office of

mediator," an office which he had in reality never assumed. The Chancellor thereupon informed the Emperor "that any explanation given by Vienna to Petersburg on the purpose and extent of Austria's measures against Serbia [which he urged Berchtold to give] could only make Russia's guilt heavier and prove it more clearly to the whole world." Thus did Bethmann Hollweg again interpret to the Emperor on July 30 the governing principles of his policy.

But the noonday hours of July 30 are important in other respects also. During these hours the Emperor received further information both on the Russian partial mobilisation and on Britain's attitude, the latter supported by a report from the naval attaché in London that "the British fleet will launch an *instant and immediate attack on us at sea* if it comes to war between us and France." This report caused the Emperor extraordinary consternation and disillusionment. He and Prince Henry had just been concocting an answer to King George, based on his first message that "we shall try all we can to keep out of this and to remain neutral." He had hoped very long that Britain would remain neutral, but when the despatches reached him — very, very belatedly — the situation changed. Their effect on Bethmann Hollweg was to cause temporary hesitations and retreats; on the Emperor it was the opposite. His naked hatred of "perfidious Albion," of "that filthy cur, Grey," of "that filthy nation of grocers" vented itself with elemental violence. "England drops the mask the moment she thinks we are safely in the corral and done for, so to speak." He now discovered who was the real war criminal, for Russia would never have been able to begin the war without England's support. "England alone is responsible for war and peace, not we any more!" The Emperor's marginal notes grow more and more sweeping. Germany is encircled; the war of annihilation has been concerted; Germany is to go under; all this is purposeful "anti-German world policy"; "and there have been people," he writes in sarcastic allusion to the Chancellor, "who have believed it possible to win over or appease England by one petty concession or another! ! ! And we have put our heads into the noose and have even introduced the slow march in our naval programme in the pathetic hope that this would placate England! ! !" Wilhelm II felt himself betrayed and double-crossed. "Edward VII dead is stronger than I am alive." At the same time, however — and this is the further and historic importance of Grey's warning and of Pourtalès' reports — his long-harboured idea turned into the conscious purpose of destroying the British Empire by unleashing revolution in the Mohammedan world.

Even before it broke out the war had ceased to be one of the traditional wars between cabinets. On July 28 Bethmann Hollweg had offered Turkey definitive terms for an alliance guaranteeing Turkey's territorial integrity *vis-à-vis* Russia if Turkey would place her army under German military command in case of war and would further bind herself to take Germany's side if Russia entered the war as a belligerent. The Austro-Serbian conflict was treated as "localised," but the whole crisis [was] viewed in the light of general war. On July 30 the negotiations were resumed more intensively with the aim of making Turkey the base for a war of revolution in the grand style against Britain. The results of this turn of policy were the surprisingly quick conclusion of a German-Turkish alliance on August 2 and the despatch of the German cruisers *Goeben* and *Breslau* to Constantinople. On July 30 and 31 preparations began to stir up revolt in the Caucasus and especially Poland, and thus to initiate the revolution against the conservative imperial power of the Romanovs which ended in the revolutionising of east-central Europe. The strategy of "utilising to the full all means of harming the enemy" which Germany, in Moltke's words, felt herself "entitled to adopt without any reservation," was consistently executed. On August 2 Moltke sketched out to Bethmann

Hollweg the outlines of Germany's plans for revolution: Turkey was to be made the basis of operations in India, Egypt and Persia, Japan was to be supported and induced to ally herself with Germany in return for recognition of the Far East as a Japanese sphere of interest, the Union of South Africa was to be subverted and Scandinavia neutralised, if not drawn into alliance with the Central Powers; similarly, the situation in the Balkans, Belgium and Italy was to be clarified without delay.

On August 5 Moltke reported to the Chancellor that the plans for insurrection in Poland had been laid, and after further allusion to "India, Egypt and also the Caucasus" (already touched on on August 2) he extended the revolutionary activity to North America. "Feeling in America," he reported, "is friendly to us; perhaps the United States may be induced to turn their navy against Britain if Canada is held out to them as the prize of victory."

First, however, the Emperor's attitude had enabled the military to begin action in Prussia and Germany. Since Russia's partial mobilisation did not yet constitute, in German eyes, sufficient ground for Germany to initiate general mobilisation, Moltke pressed Austria-Hungary to adopt instant general mobilisation without, however, declaring war on Russia, since the *casus foederis* for Germany would only arise if Russia declared war — and if Russia declared war, Moltke still believed that Britain would keep out. When, then, at 11:50 a telegram from Pourtalès revealed the *extent* of Russian partial mobilisation, the military were alerted. Nevertheless, when Bethmann Hollweg met Falkenhayn and Tirpitz at noon on the 30th, he succeeded once again in securing postponement of the proclamation of "imminent threat of war" on grounds of internal policy. Moltke, however, who had attended the meeting uninvited, now took independent action. He sent an urgent warning to Conrad to mobilise immediately against Russia (letting the dispositions against Serbia take second place) and to announce as his reason the Russian proclamation of partial mobilisation ("thus," according to Ritter, "making Russia appear the aggressor"). Only "so would the *casus foederis* for Germany arise." Britain's latest step to preserve the peace must be rejected. "To last out a European war" was "the last means of preserving Austria-Hungary." "Germany will come in under all circumstances." In the evening Moltke repeated his demands and sent the assurance that "Germany would mobilise." Szögyény reported that "till recently, all authoritative circles here had regarded the possibility of a European conflict with the most complete calm." Since July 30 signs of nervousness had become apparent, but the reason was not nervousness over the outbreak of a European war, but "anxiety lest Italy might fail to fulfil her obligations towards her partners in the Triple Alliance in the event of a general conflict." It was only because Berlin and Vienna "absolutely needed Italy if they were to be safe in entering a general conflict" that Germany was repeatedly pressing Vienna — as Moltke did twice on the 30th — to go to the limit in meeting Italy over the question of compensation.

At 9 p.m. on the 30th Bethmann Hollweg and Jagow yielded to Moltke's and Falkenhayn's insistence that the "state of imminent war" must be proclaimed by noon on the next day at the latest. At midnight, only three hours after the evening meeting, Moltke had his adjutant, von Haeften, draft the Emperor's proclamation to his people, his army and his navy. At 9 a.m. on July 31 it was agreed that the order for the measures of mobilisation consequent on this proclamation should be issued if Russia's general mobilisation was confirmed.

The report of Russia's general mobilisation was confirmed at noon on July 31. In the afternoon the Emperor, speaking from a balcony of the Palace, proclaimed a "state of imminent threat of war," declaring that "they are pressing the sword into our hand," Bethmann Hollweg's courage in waiting for Russia to order general mobilisation had thus reaped its reward: the German people was ready for war in the conviction that it had been gratuitously assailed. Sazonov had put this trump into his hand. By making Russia appear the guilty party, Bethmann Hollweg had also been able to eliminate the possibility of opposition from the Social Democrats. On the 31st Lerchenfeld reported to Munich, sarcastically but with relief, that the Social Democrats had "in duty bound, demonstrated in favour of peace," but were now "keeping quite quiet." This was also the purpose of giving Russia twelve hours' notice in the ultimatum, and of the postponement until August 1 (made possible by the perfection of her dispositions) of Germany's general mobilisation.

At the very last hour it again appeared possible that Bethmann Hollweg's policy might bear fruit and Britain remain neutral. On August 1, after the order for mobilisation had been signed, an offer arrived from London to guarantee France's neutrality. This seemed to hold out the prospect of war on a single front. The Emperor accepted the offer and ordered Moltke "to hold up the advance westward." There followed the famous scene which exposed the utter helplessness of Germany's military rigidity. Moltke protested against the Emperor's order, saying that the only up-to-date plan of campaign (the famous Schlieffen Plan, revised by him in 1913) provided for attack only against France. Nevertheless the Emperor ordered that the advance, which had already begun — patrols had penetrated into Luxemburg — was to be halted. Moltke was beside himself at the possibility of France remaining neutral and said that if the advance into France did not take place, he could "undertake no responsibility for the war." "Now," he remarked bitterly, as we know from the recollections of the Head of the Naval Cabinet, "it only remains for Russia to back out, too." After sharp argument, the Chancellor and the Chief of the General Staff ended by agreeing that the advance would have to go on "for technical reasons." Britain's offer had come too late. Yet the illusion persisted and even gathered strength.

A second telegram from Lichnowsky on the same day suggested a possibility that Britain might remain neutral even in a war between Germany and both Russia and France. "What a fabulous turn of events," reported Müller "the Emperor was delighted, and called for champagne," as was his habit later, during the war, to celebrate real or imagined victories. Bethmann Hollweg's policy seemed to have succeeded. Germany could engage Russia and France at her ease. But these hopes were to prove short-lived.

The subsequent disillusionment served to inflame still further Germany's hatred of Britain, which now became almost unbounded. On the other hand, it cleared the way for the westward advance as foreseen in the Schlieffen Plan. Italy having declared neutrality, the Germans began the World War in the face of the most unfavourable possible grouping of the powers. The declaration of war on Russia on August 1 and on France on August 3, punctilious as they were from the bureaucratic point of view and devastating as were their effects on opinion elsewhere in the world, nevertheless only marked the formal end of the complex process which had led up to them. In this respect, too, it is characteristic that Austria-Hungary's declarations of war on Russia and on the Western Powers followed only a week later, under German pressure, and that Germany's declaration of war had long since started on its journey when the Tsar telegraphed again to express confidence that peace could still be preserved in spite of the mobilisations. The violation of Belgium's neutrality enabled the British government to win over parliament and people for immediate entry into the war, a decision politically motivated by the often expressed determination not to allow Germany to overthrow France and leave Britain to face alone a continent dominated by Germany.

WHO WAS "GUILTY"?

There is no question but that the conflict of military and political interests, of resentment and ideas, which found expression in the July crisis, left no government of any of the European powers quite free of some measure of responsibility — greater or smaller — for the outbreak of the war in one respect or another. It is, however, not the purpose of this work to enter into the familiar controversy, on which whole libraries have been written, over the question of war guilt, to discuss exhaustively the responsibility of the individual statesmen and soldiers of all the European powers concerned, or to pass final judgment on them. We are concerned solely with the German leaders' objectives and with the policy actually followed by them in the July crisis, and that only in so far as their policy throws light on the postulates and origins of Germany's war aims.

It must be repeated: given the tenseness of the world situation in 1914 — a condition for which Germany's world policy, which had already led to three dangerous crises (those of 1905, 1908 and 1911), was in no small measure responsible — any limited or local war in Europe directly involving one great power must inevitably carry with it the imminent danger of a general war. As Germany willed and coveted the Austro-Serbian war and, in her confidence in her military superiority, deliberately faced the risk of a conflict with Russia and France, her leaders must bear a substantial share of the historical responsibility for the outbreak of general war in 1914. This responsibility is not diminished by the fact that at the last moment Germany tried to arrest the march of destiny, for her efforts to influence Vienna were due exclusively to the threat of British intervention and, even so, they were half-hearted, belated and immediately revoked.

It is true that German politicians and publicists, and with them the entire German propaganda machine during the war and German historiography after the war — particularly after Versailles — have invariably maintained that the war was forced on Germany, or at least (adopting Lloyd George's dictum, made for political reasons, that "we all stumbled into the war") that Germany's share of the responsibility was no greater than that of the other participants. But confidential exchanges between Germany and Austria, and between the responsible figures in Germany itself, untinged by any propagandist intent, throw a revealing spotlight on the real responsibility.

A few weeks after the outbreak of war, during the crises on the Marne and in Galicia, the Austrians asked urgently for German help against the superior Russian armies facing them. It was refused. Count Tisza then advised Berchtold to tell the Germans: "That we took our decision to go to war on the strength of the express statements both of the German Emperor and of the German Imperial Chancellor that they regarded the moment as suitable and would be glad if we showed ourselves in earnest."

Just three years later, on August 14, 1917, at the climax of a heated debate whether the war should be continued in the interest of Germany's war aims, Austria-Hungary's Foreign Minister, Count Czernin, told his German interlocutors excitedly: "It was not Austria alone that began the war then." Characteristically, the official German minutes in the Imperial Chancellery left Czernin's next sentence incomplete and passed over the retorts of the German statesmen, Michaelis, Kühlmann and Helfferich, but the minutes of the Army High Command (the OHL) gave the sentence in full: "Germany demanded that the ultimatum to Serbia should be drawn up in those sharp terms."

In February, 1918, again, Czernin asked Berchtold if he would object if he (Czernin) published a letter written by him to Tisza shortly before the outbreak of war, which showed: "what strong efforts Germany was making at that time to hold us to a hard line, and how our alliance might have been in danger if we had given way."

There is other evidence to confirm that the Central Powers in no way "slid into war." Josef Baernreither, an Austrian politician who was entirely well disposed towards the Reich and was a leading cham-

pion of the Mitteleuropa idea during the war, made the following entry on the July crisis in his diary for December, 1914:

The Germans were afraid that we would refuse to go with them if the war broke out over some question remote from us. At Algeciras we were still "seconds": later, not even that; in the Morocco crisis we did not stand by Germany firmly. But war was bound to come, as things had developed, through the faults of German and Austro-Hungarian diplomacy. So when the Sarajevo murder took place, Germany seized her opportunity and made an Austrian grievance her signal for action. That is the history of the war.

Finally, on October 8, 1919, Czernin telegraphed to Karl H. von Wiegand (the Berlin correspondent of the *Herald and Examiner*) the following reply to questions addressed to him by Wiegand:

Repeated conversations and interviews I had with Ambassador von Tschirschky could create no other impression than that his [the German] government expected warlike action on our part against Serbia. Especially a conversation I had with him during the early half of July convinced me that if we did not show this time that we were in earnest, then on the next occasion Berlin not only would not support us, but would in fact "orient" itself in some other direction.

What that would have meant for us, in view of the ethnographical composition of the Dual Monarchy and the territorial aspirations of our neighbour states, need not be explained. Tschirschky was informed about the material points in the ultimatum to Serbia before the final editing of the note and the textual contents were given to him two days before the Belgrade *démarche*.

Baernreither was confirmed in his view of the nature of the July crisis by a conversation which he had in November, 1915, with Otto Hoetzsch of Berlin, the historian of eastern Europe, leader-writer for the *Kreuzzeitung* and later German National deputy in the Reichstag. "Then" (sc., after July 5, 1914), runs the entry in Baernreither's diary, "the Emperor went off to Norway, knowing certainly that war would break out. Germany had arranged all this very cleverly, and had shown alertness and judgment in picking an occasion when she was certain of Austria's support in waging a war the inevitability of which had been becoming apparent for years past."

A week later Hoetzsch's Berlin colleague, the economist Jastrow, confirmed the correctness of Hoetzsch's view to Baernreither.

Arthur von Gwinner, Director of the Deutsche Bank, again confirmed most clearly the will to risk war which existed in Germany, especially in the Foreign Ministry, in a conversation which he had on the July crisis at the end of August, 1914, with von Capelle, the Under-Secretary of State in the Reich Naval Office. He, too, stressed the factor of Austria's unreliability:

The only reason why Lichnowsky was not informed was because here [in the Wilhelm-strasse] they were determined to force a conflict. When Capelle asked who had been the man behind this pressure, Gwinner answered, "Herr von Stumm, in the Foreign Office, for example." When Capelle expressed some doubt, he went on: "Perhaps it was a whole group. They worked systematically to get Austria committed inextricably, as the first step, so as to be sure of her. The whole plan of campaign against Serbia was arranged in advance to make a conflict inevitable."

This grave statement was published as early as 1926 by no less a man than Grand Admiral von Tirpitz, in his *Deutsche Ohnmachtspolitik* (Germany's Policy of Weakness), but it has, so far as the author knows, passed unnoticed.

Admiral Müller, commenting in his diary on the Entente's answer of December 31, 1916, to the German peace offer — a document which ascribed to Germany a substantial share of the guilt for the World War — wrote that it "contained certain bitter truths on our doings at the outbreak of the war."

Finally Albert Ballin, Bethmann Hollweg's and Jagow's intimate political confidant (he was sent to London by Jagow at the beginning of the crisis of July, 1914, in an attempt to secure Britain's neutrality, and was summoned to Berlin in the middle of 1915 to help draft Germany's note to the United States which was to decide on peace or war with America but was not received by Jagow after all), wrote at that date to the Secretary of State, out of his intimate knowledge of what had been done in July, 1914:

I make every allowance for a man who is heavily incriminated, as Your Excellency is, and has to bear the frightful responsibility for having staged this war [*für die Inscenierung dieses Krieges*] which is costing Germany generations of splendid men and setting her back 100 years.

The official documents afford ample proofs that during the July crisis the Emperor, the German military leaders and the Foreign Ministry were pressing Austria-Hungary to strike against Serbia without delay, or alternatively agreed to the despatch of an ultimatum to Serbia couched in such sharp terms as to make war between the two countries more than probable, and that in doing so they deliberately took the risk of a continental war against Russia and France. But the decisive point is that, as we now know — although for a long time it was not admitted — these groups were not alone. On July 5 and 6 the Imperial Chancellor, Bethmann Hollweg, the man in whom the constitution vested the sole responsibility, decided to take the risk and even over-trumped the Emperor when he threatened to weaken. That this was no "tragic doom," no "ineluctable destiny," but a deliberate decision of policy emerges beyond doubt from the diary of his private secretary, Kurt Riezler, who recorded in it his conversations with the Chancellor in the critical days (and, indeed, over many years). These diaries have not yet been published, but the extracts from them which have seen the light furnish irrefutable proof that during the July crisis Bethmann Hollweg was ready for war. More than this. Riezler's entry for the evening of July 8, after Bethmann Hollweg's return to Hohenfinow (where Rathenau was also stopping) shows what advance calculations the leaders of Germany were making in respect of the situation produced by the Sarajevo murder. According to his secretary, the Chancellor said: "If war doesn't come, if the Tsar doesn't want it or France panics and advises peace, we have still achieved this much, that we have manoeuvred the Entente into disintegration over this move."

In other words, Bethmann Hollweg reckoned with a major general war as the result of Austria's swift punitive action against Serbia. If, however, Russia and France were again to draw back (as in 1909 and 1911) — which he at first regarded as the less probable eventuality — then at least Germany would have achieved a signal diplomatic victory: she would have split Russia from France and isolated both without war. But war was what he expected, and how he expected its course to run we learn from his predecessor in the Chancellorship, Bülow, who had a long discussion with him at the beginning of August. Bethmann Hollweg told Bülow that he was reckoning with "a war lasting three, or at the most, four months . . . a violent, but short storm." Then, he went on, revealing his innermost wishes, it would "in spite of the war, indeed, through it," be possible to establish a friendly relationship with England, and through England with France. He hoped to bring about "a grouping of Germany, England and France against the Russian colossus which threatens the civilisation of Europe."

Bethmann Hollweg himself often hinted darkly during the war how closely Germany had been involved in the beginning of the war. He was less concerned with the "staging" of it than to register the spirit of the German leaders who had made it possible for the war to be begun even after the premises for it had collapsed. The following bitter words are taken from his address to the Central Committee of the Reichstag at the beginning of October, 1916, during the sharp debate on the initiation of unlimited submarine warfare; they outline Germany's real "guilt," her constant over-estimation of her own powers, and her misjudgment of realities:

Since the outbreak of the war we have not always avoided the danger of underestimating the strength of our enemies. The extraordinary development of the last twenty years seduced wide circles into over-estimating our own forces, mighty as they are, in comparing them with those of the rest of the world . . . in our rejoicing over our own progress [we have] not paid sufficient regard to conditions in other countries.

The July crisis must not be regarded in isolation. It appears in its true light only when seen as a link between Germany's "world policy," as followed since the mid-1890s, and her war aims policy after August, 1914.

A New War-Guilt Thesis?

GERHARD RITTER

When Gerhard Ritter, Professor of Modern European History at Freiburg, 1924–56, died on July 1, 1967, he had completed the manuscript of the fourth volume of his monumental work, *Staatskunst und Kriegshandwerk: das Problem des Militarismus in Deutschland* [*Statecraft and the Arms Profession: the Problem of Militarism in Germany*]. Although he belonged to the older generation of German historians who had lived through the war-guilt controversy of the twenties and thirties, he admitted that German war-guilt literature needed revision, but could not accept Fischer's thesis. The selection below was published in 1962 in criticism of Fischer's first edition of his book, and in some details no longer quite fits the modified English version reprinted above. Ritter, however, is less concerned with making a point-by-point criticism than in stressing the inaccuracies of interpretation and emphasis, and thus to bring out by means of illustrations the importance of approaching the sources with understanding of their meanings within their proper contexts. Is his argument convincing? Does it lead to a conclusion, or does it, rather, point the way to further study?

IT IS PART of Fischer's basic thesis that the German government, instead of seeking peace, actually considered war as necessary (in view of the development in the ratios of military strength) and saw in the July crisis of 1914 an especially favorable opportunity for a "great diplomatic success" which would push Russia completely out of the Balkans.

But was our goal really this rather than the maintenance of our Austrian ally as a great power? In other words, is the German policy of 1914 to be understood as aggressive or defensive? Around that question in the final analysis revolved the vast controversy of historians of all countries, which since 1919 has brought to light mountains of documentary sources and monographs and which Fischer again revives. Nothing can be more troublesome

and more unpleasant than to argue with him — just when one, like myself, is convinced that the older German war-guilt literature of the twenties and thirties has proved to be all too apologetic and in need of some revision. For a problem so difficult, so over-discussed, and so over-laden with source materials as the war-guilt question requires endless patience and conscientious care in the analysis of documentary evidence. Nowhere is there less room for "thesis history" than here.

Fischer explains, moreover, that he did not want to treat the war-guilt question anew, yet in fact he has done that. Only he already knew beforehand what he had to prove and proceeded into the collections of documents without being too selective.

As the first state witness for the Berlin government he brings forward a journalist,

From Gerhard Ritter, "Eine neue Kriegsschuldthese?" *Historische Zeitschrift*, v. 194 (June 1962), pp. 657–668. Translated by D. E. Lee and Stewart A. Stehlin. Footnotes have been omitted.

not a diplomat, Viktor Naumann, who as early as July 1 tried to persuade the General Secretary of the Vienna foreign ministry, Count Hoyos, to press for the attack on Serbia and promised him to work in the same sense in Berlin. Naumann was only the representative of patriotic currents of opinion in Germany, but had heard in the foreign office through Councillor von Stumm that they were greatly worried there over the rapidly growing Russian armament, and he thought (apparently correctly) that it was permissible to conclude from this and similar expressions that in the foreign office "they no longer rejected quite so completely the idea of a preventive war against Russia as they had a year before." That is really all there was to the matter. But the journalist attached to this idea political considerations concerning the necessity of risking even a European war because of Serbia, for which the Dual Alliance "was now still strong enough." That was grist for County Hoyos' mill, truly the least hesitant of all the Austrian warmongers, who then reported this conversation in detail to his minister. Fischer finds the conversation of "great significance," since Naumann's predictions were to be accurately confirmed by Germany's conduct in the July crisis. In fact they correspond accurately with the Fischer thesis. Are they, however, proof that the chancellor and the chief of the general staff wanted to unloose a preventive war?

The relation of the two allies is so portrayed by Fischer that Austrian policy was fundamentally peacefully oriented, and only through the greatest pressure by Berlin did Austria allow herself to be pushed into war. The Sarajevo assassination, so goes the account, was received in Austria with conflicting emotions, in part even with relief that the Slavophil heir to the throne had at last gone. Only a group around General Conrad had wanted to "settle accounts" with Serbia, but they were also hesitant. In contrast, from July 6, German policy, submitting without opposition to the monarchical opinions of Emperor William, pressed, not without threats concerning future alliance relations, for the strongest action even to the point of war. Now there is certainly no doubt that in Vienna they were anxious and uncertain so long as they had not made sure (through a special mission of Count Hoyos) that the German government was ready, just as in 1908 and differently than in 1912, to cover its ally in case of a conflict with Russia. From that, however, one cannot say that the initiative for the "settlement" with Serbia was forced upon the Austrians half violently by Berlin. It was they who requested support in Berlin, not vice-versa; and it means putting the course of events upside down when Fischer tries to ascribe responsibility to the German instead of the Austrian government for its disastrous diplomacy — and strategy — as lame as it was frivolous and insincere in the decisive weeks.

He obviously cannot — or will not — comprehend what the true motive was for the many Berlin admonitions advising Austria to take quick and energetic action. It was not a burning eagerness for war of some kind of militarist, but rather the very well justified fear of the dilatory half-measures of the Austrians who left their opponents time for diplomatic and military counter-measures and thereby destroyed not only the political and moral impression of the Sarajevo outrage but also the practical success of every undertaking against Serbia. Granted that German policy in the July crisis relied upon false speculation. Indeed, it had falsely evaluated almost all factors: underestimated the war preparedness of Russia and France, overestimated the impression of the outrage upon the courts of Europe and the peacefulness of English policy, and, not least, far overvalued the military capacity, political wisdom and manageability of the Austrian ally. One can even ask after that whether their basic assumption had not been faulty; whether the maintenance of the Danubian empire as a great power was still worth such a huge risk; yes, whether it was even possible in the long run, and whether this ally basically was not more trouble to us than it was worth. But the historian who asks such questions will still be aware that he therewith completely departs from a historical understanding of that period; that is, that a German statesman of 1914 could not possibly ask such questions simply because he would have compromised himself in the eyes of the German as well as the Austrian peoples. He would appear not only as a treaty-breaker, as a cowardly weakling, but even as a traitor to the German cause. For the division of 1866 had still not divided the German nation so deeply that in imperial Germany they could look with equanimity upon the ruin of the "brother empire" (whose maintenance even Bismarck had always declared a European necessity); quite apart from the fact that at this period still they considered a Russian-dominated Balkans, including Hungary, as an unbearable threat to Central Europe. Thus, even Prince Lichnowsky, our London ambassador and the sharpest critic of the Berlin government's policy, explained in a private letter to Jagow that the idea of sacrificing Austria as an ally was farthest from his mind, but he did take the view that a military "punishment" of Serbia was a thoughtless folly of Viennese policy. Today we can see that he had hit the nail on the head, that a swift military destruction of Serbia could not have solved satisfactorily the irremediable nationality problem of the Danubian monarchy, especially since their statesmen were neither united nor completely clear about what they should actually do with such a victory. At the time they believed a rapid military triumph, as a "proof of power," would strengthen once more the greatly lowered esteem of the Danubian monarchy and constrain the small Slavic neighbor folk, at least for some time. If the monarchy, however, let the Sarajevo murder, the strongest of all provocations, pass without doing anything, then its rapid decline would no longer be delayed.

But if such a powerful stroke seemed to both governments to be necessary, then the blow must fall immediately without long negotiations with other powers, and before the impression of the bloody deed at Sarajevo had evaporated throughout the world. And thus, for Berlin, it was the most terrible disappointment when little by little it turned out that the Imperial and Royal army was not in fact able to do that, not even after detailed preparations which dragged out finally until August 12 — and then denuded the Galician border of troops which thereby left Germany completely alone on the Russian front. Thus, then, the impression of almost all remarks of responsible German officials in the July weeks is that of a permanently growing and ever more severely oppressive anxiety. To overlook that and to discover some kind of desire for battle and confidence of victory is only possible with the help of radical and round-about interpretations.

One of the most curious examples of this kind of interpretation is the assertion that Under-Secretary of State Zimmermann on July 5 had "given Count Hoyos to understand" that Germany, in case of a Russian-French intervention, was able alone, because of its military position, to take on both, so that Austria-Hungary could concentrate entirely on the Balkans. To credit Zimmermann with such stupidity is to under-rate his intelligence considerably; there is not the slightest support for it in the sources. And does Fischer seriously believe that Prime Minister Count Stürgkh's anxiety that Austria would lose Germany's support in the future through feeble hesitation "refutes" the view presented from previous research that we intervened on behalf of the Danubian monarch in order not to sacrifice the last important ally?

Like the attitude of the German politicians, that of the leading military men is put entirely in a wrong light. Moltke is said to have spoken out in his last Karlsbad conversation with Conrad von Hötzendorf for a "speedy attack" and therefore had shown himself resolutely in favor of war.

Not a word about that exists in the sources. In truth the discussion was extremely serious in tone: they agreed fundamentally on how uncertain the prospects of success had become because of the defection of Rumania and the powerful preparations of Russia. Moltke was certainly greatly distressed by the prospect of Russia surpassing us in armaments even further in the coming years . . . so that "every delay meant the lessening of the chances" — a worry which he appears to have expressed many times in the summer of 1914. Fischer has completely ignored my proof that these may not be taken as eagerness for war. He appears to find somehow as striking the harmless communication of the Quartermaster General Waldersee to Jagow that he would remain quietly in his health resort, for the general staff was certainly "ready" (namely with its deployment plans and preparations for mobilization that were routinely drawn up anew every spring), for Fischer calls attention to the words "ready" and "prepared." On the same level is his interpretation of a letter in which Bethmann Hollweg, on July 16, asked the State Secretary of Alsace, Count Roedern, to prevent possible Francophobe remarks by the Alsation press; French chauvinism was not to be provoked just now, since everything depended upon the localization of the Austro-Serbian conflict. From this Fischer inferred that "the break-up of the Entente, the chief objective of pre-war diplomacy, Bethmann Hollweg now thought to force through at any price — with or without war." Can one argue any more one-sidedly?

It is peevish to cavil over such details; but it is unavoidable, for in their accumulation they distort the picture of the reality unrecognizably for the not-well-enough-informed reader — and always unfavorably for Germany. Fischer's book reports something about two dispatches of Lichnowsky from London on July 27, from which Grey's deep-seated ill-feeling over the German attitude became perceptible for the first time. Bethmann had communicated the first of these, which reported the am-

bassador's discussion with Sir Edward, to Vienna and also to the Kaiser on the very same day (for Fischer, however, the telegram is belated, namely by seven hours), and was a serious warning to Berchtold not simply to reject the English proposals. But Fischer tells of that warning only two pages later in another context, and immediately reports that the second telegram of Lichnowsky's, which contained only his personal opinion, was not circulated, so that the reader who is not informed inevitably gets the impression (and is angered by it) that the serious warning from London had simply been put in the files.

Now today it will surely occur to no one to find the attitude of Bethmann and Jagow toward the English warning politically wise and right. That up to July 29 they did not take it seriously enough and held firmly too long to the idea that they should not fail their ally and spoil for it the (apparently last) chance to establish its prestige again through a speedy military success, was a miscalculation that almost bordered on delusion. Why must the critic, however, be overcome by this mistake, while he continuously talks of intentional delay if a London despatch was debated a few hours in Berlin before being sent to Vienna, and of "suppression" of the truth, or, indeed of "falsification" if a sentence merely intended for Berlin was left out as well? Above all, why does Fischer try to exonerate the crafty policy of a Berchtold, as vacillating as it was flippant, to the disadvantage of Bethmann? I myself must repeat that I want to refute again the assertion (stemming from Albertini) that officials in Vienna after July 14 had "let it be known that they did not want it to come to extremes" and that only because of the forceful pressure from Berlin was Vienna led to its precipitate declaration of war, which was to end all attempts of the great powers at mediation. Fischer even sees the fact that Bethmann's most urgent admonitions to come to an agreement with Russia took place only on the evening of the 29th as proof that Austro-Hungarian policy "throughout was not tough and stubborn" and that in Vienna up to the 29th/30th they had not been seriously restrained, but had always been pushed forward. As proof of that he uses those additions to the Berlin telegrams in which our ambassador Tschirschky was instructed, in transmitting the London proposals "to avoid the impression that we wish to hold Vienna back," in pursuit of its goals of conclusively cutting the vital cord of the Greater Serbia propaganda, but everything had to be done to reach this goal without war, and if that should not be possible, "to improve the conditions under which we shall have to wage it, in so far as is possible."

Fischer interprets these additions as if they had intentionally pursued the objective of sabotaging the effect of the foregoing admonitions to be moderate and ready to negotiate — a very peculiar kind of diplomacy! The possibility that the additions were intended to spare the sensitivity and mistrust of the Vienna government (which always so easily felt itself patronized) and to make its compliance somehow more palatable is not once considered. For our author once for all firmly holds that Bethmann definitely did not want peace because he believed that he was obliged not to shun war, and he had now decided upon "a great diplomatic success" for Germany. The protestations of his love for peace were pure hypocrisy and likewise the warnings to Vienna were intended exclusively to push the responsibility for the war onto the Russians, whose need for prestige Fischer evidently finds to be as justified as that of the Central Powers was unjustified. Already the fact that the imperial chancellor had always emphasized in Vienna that Germany and Austria dare not appear before the world and before their own people as aggressors and as guilty of war is to him most highly suspicious; Bethmann therefore depended only upon the appearance of peace, not upon peace as such.

Up to the night of July 29/30, he had sought to deceive England through this appearance and to influence her toward neutrality — although as early as the 27th Grey had "seen through the German game." And yet in the conversation with British Ambassador Goschen, in the late evening of the 29th, Bethmann had appeared as "almost sure of victory, yes, high handed"; he had even now "revealed his goal" to the Englishman: "the first steps of German war aims, which soon after the outbreak of war appeared clearly," were the overthrow of France and Belgium, the acquisition of French colonies as a continuation of the Morocco policy of 1911, and so forth. What inconceivable folly, the reader will be compelled to say, when he learns that Bethmann Hollweg had sought to win England's consent to such plans. All the more dramatic was the effect of the sudden breakdown of all hopes of British neutrality that same night when Lichnowsky's report arrived that Grey had told him England could not remain neutral in case of a Franco-German war. But tough as ever, the chancellor held firmly to his fictions. No longer for the sake of England but for that of German Social Democracy he now rushes his last pressing admonitions and warning to Vienna (2:55 and 3:00 A.M.). The innocence of Germany and Austria must be demonstrated! It was only for that reason that he struggled so stubbornly and long against the demands of the chief of the general staff and of the war minister to answer in time the Russian mobilization, already begun, with a German counter-mobilization; the Russian total mobilization should first be awaited — for the sake of appearances! Proof of the domestic political motive (the Social Democrats) was Bethmann's remark in a meeting of the Prussian cabinet on July 30 that he believed he could rely on the loyalty of the Social Democrats in case war broke out.

Thus the impression of the chancellor's efforts (too late, to be sure) to put the brakes on the Viennese war policy even at the last moment is reduced to nothing. For that purpose, however, yet a further, almost more grotesque proof is made to serve and is emphatically underlined by our author:

Bethmann cancelled his dispatch to Vienna on the evening of July 30, about nine o'clock, which contained a new, quite unequivocal admonition to come to an understanding with Russia, by a new telegram at 11:20 P.M., because at 11:08 (!) a rather unimportant dispatch from the King of England to Prince Henry had arrived which appeared to offer a new "glimmer of hope" for English neutrality — and therefore made stopping the war unnecessary!

Does not Fischer know the true reason, namely that significant conference of the chancellor with Moltke and Falkenhayn on the late evening of July 30, the tragic turning point of the whole July crisis, in which the generals convinced the resisting chancellor that it was already too late for mediation attempts and negotiations with the Russians, since according to the information of the general staff Russian total mobilization was already obviously in progress? Their apprehensions were confirmed, moreover, in the course of the night. Nevertheless Fischer appears not to believe the genuineness of these reasons. Rather, he maintains offhandedly that an excited marginal note of the Emperor on a dispatch from Petersburg, which revealed Russian partial mobilization against Austria, had removed all the previous inhibitions . . . as if eagerness for war and not burning anxiety concerning the well-timed execution of the now rigidly fixed Schlieffen plan had prevailed at the general staff! Whoever reads the sources soberly and without bias can only shake his head at such a contrived interpretation.

Naturally the true reason for the nervous pressure of Moltke for the total mobilization of Austria on July 29/30 remains completely misunderstood — as completely misunderstood as in the older war-guilt literature up to Albertini. Fischer has taken no notice of my pains to clear up the military-technical relationships. Instead, he piles up fictitious arguments in order to read into the German policy of July motives of imperialistic power and conquest. If Bethmann, for example, already bestirred himself from July 28 over an alliance with Turkey, then, according to Fischer, he purposely widened the local war to a world war. Moltke's memorandum of August 2, a politically rather naive concoction, in which he recommended to the foreign office the revolutionizing of half the world against England, is cited in detail. Obviously it also serves as proof that in Berlin the war from the beginning was understood to be not defensive, but aggressive, yes, as a revolutionary act, as a *Griff nach der Weltmacht* [grab for world power].

Moltke's attitude immediately before the outbreak of the war is generally pictured in a way for which the expression "biassed" seems to me altogether too mild. One knows that he fell into despair when the Emperor on the evening of August 1 suddenly ordered him to stop the war in the west, which had already begun, because a remarkable telegram (quickly recognized as an error) of Lichnowsky's for a moment rekindled the hope that England would guarantee French neutrality if we renounced the idea of attacking in the west. Moltke's excitement over this unexpected disruption of his plan and over the presumptuous demand of the Emperor to turn the whole deployment toward the east, I myself have characterized as a personality failing (similar to that of Falkenhayn and Tirpitz). But there can be no doubt at all about what gave rise to this excitement: the general staff did not believe, any more than the war minister did, that France would actually keep still and considered Lichnowsky's report (correctly so) as a soap bubble. Had Moltke followed the Emperor's command, it would only have led to awful chaos; besides Moltke got a most ungracious reception of his remonstrance by William II and the latter's just as careless as dilettantist interference in strategic decisions seemed to be evidence of distrust that deeply shocked him. No one who can read the sources impartially will understand his exclamation at this moment, "Now, it only remains for Russia to back out, too!" which was recorded by

Admiral Müller (in a greatly shortened note), as anything other than bitter irony. Fischer, who asserts that the Chief of the General Staff was "beside himself over the possibility of a neutral France," suggests to the reader that he was just as frightened over a "backing out of Russia" — therefore frightened (what should one infer otherwise than that?) over the maintenance of peace.

After all that, it is hardly rewarding to argue with Fischer's concluding considerations concerning "who was guilty," in which he seeks to support his thesis by the later retrospective views of Tisza, Czernin, Admiral von Müller, Ballin, and Bethmann Hollweg, which he interprets as either a kind of confession of guilt, or as accusations by well-informed participants. He does not speak exactly of Germany's sole guilt, but says, cautiously and informally, that "the governments of the participating European powers in one way or another and in very different degrees shared in the responsibility for the outbreak of the World War." Since in his exposition, however, there is not a syllable about the co-responsibility of the non-German powers, it seems to me as good as excluded that any reader will interpret this background of the war as something other than a renewal of the guilt clause of Versailles. A completely new picture of Chancellor Bethmann Holl-weg is put before us. In place of a very conscientious, honest, but in his decisions changeable official who was always beset by fresh doubts and was lacking in a sure political instinct, there appears a tough and crafty power-politician who plays with the fate of Germany with unscrupulous flippancy (one can hardly call it anything else). And this impression is accumulated massively throughout the main part of the book, and is strengthened by documents from the time of the World War, always interpreted in the same sense.

In summary, let it be said that this work for the first time has applied the thesis of Ludwig Dehio (which is as glittering as it is dangerous and is in the last analysis only a half-truth) concerning the "war for hegemony" as the essence of both world wars, in a great exposition from the sources. At the same time in Fischer a first peak is reached in today's fashionable stream of political history — the obscuring of Self in German historical consciousness that, since the catastrophe of 1945, has superseded the earlier apotheosis of Self, and now appears successfully and one-sidedly to assert itself. I am convinced that it will work out not less fatefully than the superpatriotism of former times. Thus I lay the book down not without genuine sadness — sadness and anxiety respecting the coming generation.

SUGGESTIONS FOR ADDITIONAL READING

The published sources and the studies on the general background of the First World War and the crisis of July, 1914, have reached vast proportions. By selecting a few of the more general works and perhaps some of the monographs and primary sources a student may gain a deeper insight into the international relations and the diplomacy that preceded the outbreak of the war.

Among the older general works, those of Brandenburg and Fay, from which extracts have been printed above, will repay reading. They are not far apart in their interpretation, although Brandenburg is much more detailed on the period after 1890. For a thorough grounding in the years from 1870 to 1902, which saw the creation of the major alliance systems and the height of imperialistic rivalry, William L. Langer's *European Alliances and Alignments, 1870–1890* (New York, 1933) and *The Diplomacy of Imperialism* (New York, 1935, 2 v.) give the complete story and also provide excellent critical bibliographies. There is nothing to match them for the period after 1901, but the two volumes of George Peabody Gooch, *Before the War* (London, New York, Toronto, 1936–38) approach these years in a novel way by describing the policy of each of the major foreign ministers. Specific crises have been well treated by Eugene N. Anderson, *The First Morocco Crisis* (Chicago, 1930), Bernadotte E. Schmitt, *The Annexation of Bosnia, 1908–1909* (New York, 1937), Ima C. Barlow, *The Agadir Crisis* (Chapel Hill, N. C., 1940), and Ernst Helmreich, *Diplomacy of the Balkan Wars, 1912–1913* (Cambridge, Mass., 1938). Two excellent shorter works which will serve as an introduction to the whole period are Bernadotte E. Schmitt, *Triple Alliance and Triple Entente* ("Berkshire Studies," New York, 1934) and Alfred F. Pribram, *England and the International Policy of the European Great Powers, 1871–1914* (Oxford, 1931). An especially valuable textbook, which deals briefly with the backgrounds of the First World War is C. E. Black and E. C. Helmreich, *Twentieth Century Europe* (3rd ed., New York, 1966).

Of the more recent literature, which in the main tends to take an anti-revisionist attitude toward the role of Germany and to lay greater emphasis upon power politics, Nicholas Mansergh, *The Coming of the First World War: a Study in European Balance, 1878–1914* (London, New York, Toronto, 1949), provides a good and relatively brief introduction. More recent surveys are those of Pierre Renouvin, *Histoire des relations internationales . . . De 1871 à 1914*, and A. J. P. Taylor, *Struggle for Mastery in Europe*, from which extracts have been reprinted above. The first volume of the work of the Italian journalist and scholar Luigi Albertini, *Origins of the War of 1914* (New York, 1952–57, 3 v.), covers the period from 1878 to June, 1914. A shorter and more readable survey, which emphasizes the disintegration of Austria-Hungary as a contributing factor to the coming of the war, is that of Laurence Lafore, *The Long Fuse* (Philadelphia and New York, 1965). The most recent attempt to digest the literature on the backgrounds of the war, as well as its significance, is by D. F. Fleming, *The Origins and Legacies of World War I* (Garden City, 1968).

On the July crisis of 1914, besides Fay's second volume and the other works on the revisionist side from which selections have been reproduced above, Alfred von Wegerer, *A Refutation of the Versailles War Guilt Thesis* (New York, 1930) is an outstanding product of the German foreign office section which directed scholarly revisionist propaganda. In opposition to the revisionist view are Pierre Renouvin, *The Immediate Origins of the War* (New

Haven, 1928) and the monumental work of Bernadotte E. Schmitt, *The Coming of the War* (New York and London, 1930, 2 v.). Professor Schmitt has written a valuable postscript to his book, in which he takes account of material appearing in the 1930's: "July 1914: Thirty Years After," *Journal of Modern History*, XVI (September 1944), 169–204. This article, together with the pamphlet *The Origins of the First World War* (London, 1958), from which excerpts have been printed above, might well serve as an introduction to further reading. Jules Isaac, *Un Débat Historique: Le Problème des Origines de la Guerre* (Paris, 1933), has made a judicious but vigorous comparison, principally of Fay's and Schmitt's works on the origins of the war, and has indicated clearly the areas of agreement and disagreement.

Although the Sarajevo crime has tended to recede into the background of literature on the outbreak of the war, its implications for Serbian and even Austro-Hungarian and Russian guilt, as well as the tangled story of the plot itself, have been thoroughly if not exhaustively explored. The two "classics" with diametrically conflicting views are: Edith Durham, *The Sarajevo Crime* (London, 1925), and R. W. Seton-Watson, *Sarajevo: — a Study in the Origins of the Great War* (London, 1926). More recently, Joachim Remak, *Sarajevo: the Story of a Political Murder* (London, New York, 1959), has rewritten in very readable fashion the story of the plot and what happened to the participants. The most exhaustive treatment of the backgrounds of the plot and a detailed examination of the question of the guilt of Serbia, Austria-Hungary, and Russia is that of Vladimir Dedijer, *The Road to Sarajevo* (New York, 1966; London, 1967). He comes to a conclusion that largely confirms the position of Seton-Watson, namely that the plot is to be explained mainly in terms of Bosnian grievances and aspirations.

Since conflicting opinions often arise from differing interpretations of key documents, the serious student will want to examine for himself some of the primary source material, but even if equipped with the necessary language facility will not find it possible to peruse the voluminous collections of diplomatic documents published by the Austrian, British, French, German, Italian, Russian, and other governments. A good selection of documents during the July crisis is that of Imanuel Geiss, *July 1914: the Outbreak of the First World War* (New York, 1967), with lengthy introductory notes and a conclusion, both of which follow the Fischer thesis. The German original, *Julikrise und Kriegsausbruch 1914* (Hannover, 1963–64, 2 v.) is much more complete, containing over six times as many documents. The original publications in "color books" on the July crisis of 1914 have been conveniently collected by the British Government in *Collected Diplomatic Documents Relating to the Outbreak of the European War* (London, 1915) and by James Brown Scott for the Carnegie Endowment for International Peace in *Diplomatic Documents Relating to the Outbreak of the European War* (New York, 1916, 2 v.).

The multitudinous memoirs or biographies of statesmen, diplomats, generals, and journalists are more enjoyable reading and offer more insight into personalities and attitudes. All the leading foreign ministers or prime ministers of the immediate prewar years have published apologias excepting Count Aehrenthal and Count Berchtold of Austria-Hungary, but recently a full-length study of Berchtold has helped to fill the gap: Hugo Hantsch, *Leopold Graf Berchtold: Grand Seigneur und Staatsmann* (Graz, Wien, Köln, 1963). The memoirs vary greatly in value and interest. Among the best are British Prime Minister Asquith, *The Genesis of the War* (London, 1923), Sir Edward Grey, *Twenty-five Years* (New York, 1925, 2 v.), Prince von Bülow, *Memoirs* (Boston, 1931–32, 4 v.), Chancellor Bethmann-Hollweg, *Reflections on the World War* (London, 1920), Prince Lichnowsky, *Heading for the Abyss* (London, 1928), Raymond Poincaré, *Au Service de la France* (Paris, 1926–1933, 10 v.), of which the first four volumes up to the outbreak of the war have been translated and adapted by Sir George Arthur, *The Memoirs of Raymond Poincaré, 1912,* and *1913–1914* (London, 1926–28, 2 v.).

For the fullest and most detailed treatment of the July crisis, see Albertini's second and third volumes of the work cited above. He deals with all the powers and has made a most convincing case against Germany, whose responsibility he puts even above Austria's. His text is so interlarded with direct quotations from the documents, moreover, that it provides an excellent introduction to the huge body of primary sources. As yet the "Fischer controversy" is mostly confined to German publications, although the 3rd edition of his book, *Griff nach der Weltmacht* (Düsseldorf, 1964), has been translated in shortened form, as noted in the introduction to the selection reprinted above. His thesis is well set forth in Geiss's introductions and conclusions to the selected documents in *July 1914,* cited among the collections of documents. A number of essays, including comments on Fischer's thesis, first issued in the *Journal of Contemporary History,* I, 3 and 4 (1966), was reissued in *1914: the Coming of the First World War,* edited by Walter Laqueur and George L. Mosse (New York, 1966). The first two years of the debate in Germany is well represented in *Deutsche Kriegsziele, 1914–1918,* edited by Ernst W. Graf Lynar (Frankfurt/M and Berlin, 1964). An interesting book which was written in 1923 but was suppressed because of its anti-revisionist tone is Hermann Kantorowicz, *Gutachten zur Kriegsschuldfrage,* edited by Imanuel Geiss (Frankfurt/M, 1967). Robert A. Kann has given the character and conclusions of the book in a lengthy

review, *Central European History,* I (1968), 383–389.

Among the available bibliographies, an unusually informative and critical guide to the memoirs and other sources provided by actors in the drama of 1914 is George Peabody Gooch, *Recent Revelations of European Diplomacy* (4th ed., revised and enlarged, London, New York, Toronto, 1940). Annotated bibliographies are provided in *Foreign Affairs Bibliography, 1922–1932,* edited by W. L. Langer and H. F. Armstrong (New York, 1933), *1932–1942,* edited by Robert Gale Woolbert (New York, 1945), and *1942–1952,* edited by Henry L. Roberts and others (New York, 1955). A useful listing of both articles and books, but without comment, may be found in Lowell J. Ragatz, *A Bibliography for the Study of European History, 1815–1939* (Ann Arbor, Michigan, 1941) and three supplements (1943, 1945, and 1956). Finally, the best single handbook for further study and research is the ninth volume, by Pierre Renouvin and others, of the "Clio" series: *L'époque contemporaine,* part 2, *La paix armée et la grande guerre, 1871–1919* (Paris, 1953), while the most complete and detailed guide to publications up to 1941 in all languages on the origins of World War I is the monthly periodical devoted to the "war guilt" question, *Die Kriegsschuldfrage: Berliner Monatshefte für Internationale Aufklärung,* edited by Alfred von Wegerer (Berlin, 1923–1941). Obviously, however, none of these bibliographical aids covers recent literature or the "Fischer controversy." For both, Fischer's *Germany's Aims in the First World War,* Geiss's *July 1914,* and *Deutsche Kriegsziele* provide extensive bibliographical lists.